‘It’s

The ‘dark art’ of police humour

Volume II

By

Michael Layton & Stephen Burrows

First published by Bostin Books in 2020

Find us on our Website www.bostinbooks.co.uk and our Facebook page ‘Bostin Books’

DEDICATION

To family, friends and former colleagues who have supported us on our writing journey and those retired police officers who have assisted us in keeping the history of policing in the West Midlands and UK in general alive.

Since we wrote this book we have discovered that the word 'Blag' has been registered as a Trademark (who would have thought you could own the word 'Blag'?) So if you're reading this in the UK or in the USA, you will be pleased to hear that the TM holder is a huge fan of law enforcement and was delighted to grant us permission".

Other books by Michael Layton and Stephen Burrows

Joint:

Historical Crime Fiction:

Black Over Bill's Mother's – A Storm is Coming
Keep Right On
The Touch Of Innocence

Non-Fiction:

One in For D & D – a little book of police slang
It's A Blag – police tricks and funny stories
Ta-Ra A Bit, Our Kid – a little book of slang used by 'Brummies'
Reporting for Duty – West Midlands Police (The first twenty-five years 1974 – 1999)
Top Secret Worcestershire
The Noble Cause
Walsall's Front Line – Volume 1 (1997-1998)
Walsall's Front Line – Volume 2 (1998-1999)

By Michael Layton

Non-Fiction:

Hunting the Hooligans (With Robert Endeacott)
Tracking the Hooligans (With Alan Pacey)
Police Dog Heroes (With Bill Rogerson)
Birmingham's Front Line
Violence in the Sun
The Night the Owl Cried - A Taste of Cyprus (With Androulla Christou-Layton)
The Hooligans Are Still Among Us (With Bill Rogerson)

By Stephen Burrows

Historical Fiction

Pretty Thing

Introduction

These stories are a mix of humour and tricks, but also bring to life the police service of the past. The days when the world was perhaps a little more innocent, simpler, and definitely not 'politically correct' The words of this contributor might assist the reader's understanding,

"Great days. When I first joined the job and got blagged a couple of times, I got a bit 'pissed off' about it. A wise old 'dogman' said, bobbies don't blag people they don't like, if they're blagging you, they're accepting you." A truer word was never spoken.'

We have left these tales in the words of those involved rather than 'sanitising' them as we think they add something more than humour, a record of policing history that would otherwise fade away.

Names have been removed where appropriate to protect the innocent and guilty. Please suspend the temptation to apply modern values. This was the reality….

The Stories

'Biting the bullet'

'I worked with a young PCSO at Lye, he was only 19 years old when he joined, a very nice lad. He had a bad habit of chewing the end of pens, and several colleagues commented on it.

He was that 'fresh' he was always going to swallow any 'blag' (practical joke) that was played on him. One day he went out on patrol, so I typed out a white report - *'From Sergeant A to PCSO B. It has come to my attention that you have been seen chewing the ends of various police-issue pens. I must inform you that those pens are police property and that any damage done to them is in fact an offence of criminal damage. Please refrain from chewing pens. If there are any further instances of criminal damage, I shall have no choice but to record it as a crime and investigate you. Please sign below to acknowledge that you have received and understand this warning.'*

He came back in from patrol with his colleague and saw the report in his basket. He picked it up and began to read it. As he did so I picked up a BIC biro and began chewing on the end, crushing bits of plastic in my mouth. The whole office was watching. "What's that?" I asked. "It's a report from the sergeant, I've got to stop chewing pens or I'll be prosecuted" he replied. "What!" I replied and spat bits of pen everywhere "that's outrageous." I then continued to chew my pen.

"Well I've signed it" he said "I didn't realise it was so serious."...'

*

'Childish behaviour'

The same PCSO did however get considerably more streetwise in the following years. A couple of years later a couple of PCSO colleagues came back from a local primary school with about fifty pictures that the children had done. The theme was 'Don't Drop Litter' and the children had been asked to do an A3 sized poster. I looked through them, some had been done by older children, some by very young children. I asked the PCSO's for a piece of paper and some felt tips pens.

In red pen on the back I wrote in 'unjoined', teacherly type writing *"Please forgive Jonathan's language officers, he suffers from Tourette's syndrome."* I then did a poster showing a young boy dropping a Coke can. Beside him is a bobby in full uniform with a voice bubble saying *"Fukin (sic) pick it up."* I had the child wearing Nike trainers and I threw in an irrelevant hedgehog (hegog)(sic) because kids do that.

Loads of bobbies who came in that day including the Inspector 'had it', thinking it was real. My PCSO walked in, saw it, pointed at me and said, "He's done that." So, he did learn!'

*

'Boots are made for walkin'

‘On another occasion an officer bought a brand-new pair of boots, but before he could open the box, he went off long-term sick. One day I found myself needing a pair of boots and didn’t expect him to ever come back, so I helped myself. He came back to work about nine months later and couldn’t find his boots, so I kindly spent the best part of his first shift back helping him turn Lye ‘nick’ upside down looking for them whilst they were sat nice and snug on my feet!’

*

‘Friday the 13th?’

‘I remember one day the Sergeant told me and another officer we were doing a warrant, but we had other plans, so knowing how superstitious he was we came up with a plan to tell him at separate times that we’d had a dream that we’d done the warrant and the place was booby-trapped and we all died. He cancelled the warrant.’

*

‘Trust me, I’m a Policeman’

‘I was at Lye talking to two officers one day. I told them that another officer had the loosest lips in the universe. "If you want everyone to know something" I said, "just tell him and swear him to secrecy, before long everyone will know."

"Is he that bad?" they asked. "Too right he is", I replied. They left whilst I carried on doing a committal file for court.

About an hour later the officer I had been talking about walked in and asked me if I wanted a cup of tea. He then promptly started telling me how one of the officers was having an affair with our female Inspector.

A short time later the other two walked in and the two of them fell about laughing. They had left Lye and gone to Stourbridge where they had bumped into their 'victim' and had 'blagged' him and sworn him to secrecy not to tell anyone that one of them was having it off with the Inspector. He promised faithfully not to say anything and promptly came to the station and told me.'

*

'The early bird..'

'One of our Sergeants at Lye liked a drop of wine in the evenings. Sometimes he'd be down to start work at 8am and he'd roll in at tennish and work a 10am – 6pm instead.

A few months later a new Chief Superintendent started, a Northern Irishman. We were all occasionally guilty of rolling into work five minutes late, so one day I spoke to my younger colleagues and said

"New gaffers like to get out and visit the nicks on their division. For the next few weeks make sure that you turn up on time because you don't want to turn up ten minutes late and find the new Chief Superintendent here."

The Sergeant agreed with me. About a week later he was due to work an 8am – 4pm. One of my colleagues asked me to help her arrest a guy who was appearing at Birmingham Magistrates Court.

Before I left at 9am I wrote the name of the Chief Superintendent and my mobile phone number on a piece of paper and told a colleague, “When the Sergeant gets in tell him that when you arrived at work at 8am this morning the Chief Superintendent and Inspector were here waiting for you. They asked the whole office about their vision of Neighbourhood Policing and the contribution that they could make. They spoke about their ambitions for the Division. Before they left the Chief Superintendent looked at the postings board and asked where you were.”

At about 10am I was at Birmingham Magistrates Court when my phone started ringing. I answered in my best Northern Irish accent.

"Ah hello Sir, Sergeant ……….. from Lye Police Station" came the reply. "Ah hello Sergeant!" I said. "I came to Lye this morning to introduce myself to your staff, but you weren't there. The postings board shows you as working an 8am – 4pm today. Where were you at 8am please?"

The Sergeant began telling me about a terrible problem that was being experienced with off-road motorcyclists riding around the Wollescote area during the early evening. "I am pedal cycle trained so I'm going over there at about 4.30pm in the hope that I can spot them." "That's very commendable" I said. "Thank you Sir" he replied.

"However," I went on, "Why did you not update the postings to show your shift change?" "An oversight Sir, I'm very sorry, it won't happen again" he replied.

"Very well" I said "Now before I go, PC (me) is one of your officers, isn't he?" "Yes Sir" came the response.

"Can you look on his 'Docutrak' please, there is a crime report on there for a theft from dwelling."

The Sergeant found it. I should add at this stage that a Chief Superintendent wouldn't have a bloody clue about 'Docutrak', I was just relishing the moment. "Can you please forward that to DC Hatfield because apparently he has cleared that offence."

The Sergeant forwarded the enquiry.

"Have you done that Sergeant?" I asked. "Yes, Sir I've just sent that" he replied.

"Cheers" I said in my own voice.

Cue much swearing, as various colleagues burst through his office door taking the piss out of him.'

*

'A walk on the wild side'

'Here's one that I was told some time ago by a friend who was ex-RAF. It was a frequently played blag apparently. The military aircraft in question has two doors in the roof area of the fuselage. You had to climb a small ladder to access these. One was towards the front of the aircraft, the other towards the rear. There was a bulkhead or 'wall' dividing the two.

Experienced flight-staff sometimes had to take large groups of young airmen up in this plane. One of the crew would pick on a young 'newbie' and say, "I'm just going to pop up onto the top of the aircraft to check something out, make sure they don't take off without telling me." He'd then climb up the ladder, open the door onto the top of the plane, someone else would then lock and secure it. He'd then walk along the roof of the plane and drop down through the other door into the forward part of the aircraft.

The 'newbie' who had a million and one things to think about would sometimes forget what he had been told. The plane would take off, fly around for half an hour then return to the airfield. When the engines were turned off the crew member would climb out of the forward door, walk along the roof having doused himself in water and made himself look rather dishevelled and begin banging on the rearmost door.

Another crew member would open it and he would drop inside looking rather windswept. He would confront the youngster saying, "I told you to tell them what I was doing, I've been clinging on for dear life up there!'

*

'Sweet thing'

'When I was a Permanent Beat Officer on the 'B' Division we ran a 'First Night Watch' (6pm x 2am) van once a month with a Sergeant in charge. We always went to 'Eric's' Chinese in Cotteridge and ate the grub in the van around 8pm.

One of our number always had the same order, which included a frittered pineapple. Now the blag begins ....I also included this sweet dish in my order that night and the Sergeant carefully removed the pineapple from the other officer's order and hid it in the van.

So later at our grub time he realised his sweet was missing and started to get upset .... very upset, he was driver and sitting in the driving seat.

He then saw I was eating a frittered pineapple and put two and two together, omg! Did he lose it. He spent the rest of the night driving around like a 'nutter' and swearing revenge and quoting the Theft Act.

At the end of the shift he went into the nick to book off, not speaking to any of us, we stayed outside and awaited his return. He eventually came out into the Bournville car park and went to his car, where he found his pineapple fritter on the driving seat.

He quietly drove out of the car park without looking in our direction, we were crying with laughter. Next day he put his hands up and admitted it was a great blag'.

*

'Wish you were here?'

'When I was on the Regional Crime Squad, we had a senior officer who started to get really worried about the amount of money we were spending on expenses and was always onto us to reduce costs. One day we followed a target all the way down to Dover and left him as he got on a ferry to cross to France. Before the ferry left though we asked a passenger to post a card for us when he got to France. It said *'Still following the target and currently in Paris. See you soon'*. It was addressed to the senior officer who went ballistic when he received it.'

*

'Quick thinking'

‘The long serving office-man at a small police station just outside Birmingham City Centre liked his ‘liquid lunches’ from the pub across the road. One evening he locked the front door of the station, took a radio with him and went across the road for a ‘quick one’.

A new Superintendent turned up at the station for a visit and couldn’t get in. The office-man was called on the radio as to his whereabouts and he managed to sneak back into the station via a side-door from the vehicle pound next to the station. On opening the front door from the inside for the Superintendent he announced that he had been checking on the security of the cars in the compound and shut the station door to prevent people wandering in.

He was commended by the Superintendent for his actions!’

*

‘Mushroom picking’

‘During the Miner’s Strike I was a DC at Bridge St West and used to taxi the very tired Beat Officers back to their houses.

During this time another CID officer took the CID Allegro car for a prison visit, leaving me to ‘hold the fort’.

They later broke down and limped into the police motorway post at Corley Services and I was tasked to take a Metro down to allow them to carry on.

Some Traffic Officers found the water pump to be leaking and filled her up then told me to drive gently back to the police garage, but not on the M6, and they led me off the motorway through the back roads and I joined the A45 on the edge of Coventry.

I got as far as fifty yards before the junction with the A452 roundabout and it seized in the outside lane. Not a great place to be with drivers speeding up then seeing the CID car and having to swerve at the last minute.

I popped the bonnet up, left the flashers going and could see a row of toilets and a red telephone box.

Remember, I am in my fourth year of policing Brum, from the City Centre Division and have no idea about anywhere outside the City as I'm from Scotland.

So off to the phone box I go. No change in my pocket and I have to call 999. I did notice a lot of cars parked in the toilet's layby with their bonnets up and surmised they all needed water.

There were a few blokes walking around with plastic bags with what looked like an LP inside. I explained my predicament, didn't know if I was in West Midlands or Warwickshire and said, 'sorry please ring 999', as I had no money.

They were as 'good as gold' and told me to wait by the box for a return call.

I did and a male came up to me and asked if I wanted help "looking for mushrooms" to which I said no, I had broken down.

He smiled and didn't walk too far and shortly after Park Lane rang to say recovery was on the way. As I walked back to the CID car my friend was smiling at me and followed me with his eyes.

As I was by the car there were van loads of Special Patrol Group and other 'call signs' passing, beeping and shouting abuse as CID cars were all consecutive numbers in the West Midlands and easy to spot.

One crew stopped and then bumped the car onto the offside verge which was hard standing making it safer. At the same time taking the mick about me looking for a 'cottage'. I didn't understand any of it but was glad of the safer position now.

Off they went and more vans passed with more abuse and I could still see my friend in the trees by the toilets then I saw others!!!!

Suddenly it dawned on me what this all was, and I was straight in that car, doors locked, warrant card and vehicle logbook propped up in the window.

When the crew turned up, they were laughing their heads off and I told them about the mushroom request and that made them laugh even louder. All through my career whenever the one lad saw me, he would just say "Mushrooms" and wink at me.

I never told anybody what that was all about! - until now...'

*

'A nasty dose'

'About 1971, members of a shift at Steelhouse Lane were part of a football trip to play brother officers in Frankfurt, Germany.

The match took place and was thoroughly enjoyed by all. I do not remember the final score. There followed immense hospitality by the Frankfurt Police, culminating in a visit to a local brothel.

One Birmingham officer who was an ex-cadet, and only a few months into service, was known to be a virgin. Be assured that the rest of his Unit were determined to ensure he 'broke his duck', which he duly did. It did, however, backfire on the lads in so much that instead of quietly savouring the moment, the officer then kept on about his newfound sexual prowess and bored the pants off everyone on the journey home.

Revenge was required. A reasonable gap of a couple of weeks was allowed; then the plan was enacted. One officer had obtained some official Frankfurt Polizei headed notepaper and a letter was fabricated purporting to come from the Commisar of Polizei, Frankfurt-am-Mein to support a 'blag' on the officer.

During the next set of nights, and in a lull in usual hostilities with errant citizens of 'Brummagem', the 'victim' was summoned to see the watch Inspector, who informed the officer a letter had been received from Frankfurt and the content thanked the officers for attending their City and playing football, and for enjoying the splendid night out afterwards, including the visit to the local authority licensed bordello.

The letter went on to assure that this was a well-run and regulated establishment, and that rigorous and frequent health checks were applied to the ladies concerned. However, one of the ladies was discovered to have contracted a sexually transmitted disease known as 'STREPTOCOCCI EPIDIDIMOUS'.

All contacts of the girl had been traced, save the young officer and it was suggested he sought medical attention.

At this stage I would add that this was such a well-planned 'blag', the Unit had taken the staff at Ward 19 – the Special Clinic at the General Hospital, into the deception, and they were all geared up to receive him and put him through the 'mincer'.

However he took it so badly when he had the letter read to him, and was likened to a 'frightened rabbit' caught in car headlights, it was thought best to cut short the 'blag' and put him out of his misery as it were.

I still laugh about it all these years later.'

*

'Buying the farm'

'I lived in Oscott School Lane in the late 80's and one winter evening I went out to walk down to my parent's house on the Beeches Estate. It was dark and after 7pm (I know that because the local shops were shut.).

At the end of my road I met a young policeman who was on foot. He asked me where the nearest phone box was, so I presume his radio wasn't working.

I directed him to the shops, and he walked off much faster than I could go.

When I got to the shops the same policeman was standing looking lost and perplexed. He asked me if there was a farm around there – of course there wasn't.

He said he had to go to Brooklyn Farm to find out about a break-in.

Now, Brooklyn Farm had been pulled down some thirty-odd years before and Brooklyn Technical College occupied the site.

It was obvious he was out on a fool's errand and I told him so.

At that time, I knew the name of the last owner of the farm because there was a huge painting of her, and her brothers, on the back wall of St. Matthews Church Hall so I told him to go back to whoever has sent him and tell them that he had spoken to the lady, and gave him her name, and her brothers and there hadn't been a break in.

He looked both relieved and 'fuming' and went back the way he had come. Probably heading for Kingstanding Police Station.'

*

'Suits you Sir!'

'I popped into 'Rackhams' Store when I was doing diplomatic protection for the Indian high Commissioner. They'd got a sale on for sports jackets, so I nipped in during my dinner break.

I'm just looking at a nice one when the assistant comes up behind me and asks me if he can help. When I say I'm just looking at this particular jacket he reaches up and slips off my jacket.

After a couple of seconds, I click why everything has stopped dead and everyone is looking at me. I'd forgotten I'd got a shoulder holster on and was carrying a Beretta!

I frantically got my warrant card out and told everyone it was okay, and I was a police officer and hoping no one had phoned Steelhouse Lane.

I got my jacket back on and legged it back to the High Commission. I'm sat there all quiet, listening to the radio and pleased that no one has been called to Rackhams.

I was asked by the rest of the team why I was quiet and eventually 'coughed' what had happened. One of the team then said "Blimey, you'd think they'd be used to it, so and so did it last year, I did it the year before!"…'

*

'The Scottish play'

'Sometime in 1993 myself and an Indian colleague were sent, post haste, to Aviemore to collect a prisoner. It was in the days when we collected detainees wanted on warrant.

Having arrived there after closing time we found somewhere open late for libation. The place was called 'The Red McGregor' and was the local SNP stronghold.

Deciding that English accents might not be accepted too warmly my partner became a cousin to the Aga Khan and I was his American bodyguard. The locals lapped it up, hook, line and sinker.

With a roll of 'Fivers' (from an advance of expenses) every time we needed more drinks, he would produce the cash with a flourish, gabble something indistinctly in Punjabi and I would take the cash and buy beer.

The locals were so convinced by our act that we were even offered first 'dibs' on the local dealer's cocaine due in the very next day from Aberdeen!

The following morning, armed with a boot full of the local butcher's offerings of Haggis and Mealie-pudding (requested by EVERY 'Jockanese' officer on the home patch), we collected our prisoner and headed back.

To end the story, we paraded as usual following our return and dished out the butcher's delights. An officer, young in years and known for being quite naive, enquired as to exactly WHAT was a Haggis? Unprompted, and very convincingly, myself and a female colleague went into this long 'spiel' about it being the closest thing to a direct hybrid of mammal and fowl that lived amongst the gorse and heather of the Highlands. We even came up with a spoof Haggis Season opening day akin to the Glorious Twelfth!

Said gullible officer believed it 100%. - she later went on to become a Chief Superintendent, so it goes to show that intelligence should not be confused with 'nous'! ....'

*

'If you want to know the time ask a ....'

'Pre 1974, during my days in Single Men's Quarters at Steelhouse Lane, there was a PC in living there who was the permanent office constable at Bordesley Green Police station some 3.3 miles away.

He was very much a 'creature of habit' and an avid clock watcher, a fact known to his fellow residents.

When on 'first day watch', 6am to 2pm, he would get to work at about 05.20hrs and relieve his colleague on nights and the following shift would reciprocate. Office men all over Birmingham City Police did this and it helped to smooth the handover.

His habit would be; get up with the alarm about 04.15hrs, wash and get into uniform, a quick 'cuppa', walk downstairs and past the station office, noting the time as 04.47hrs and out into Steelhouse Lane. He would then walk up to Colmore Row passing the Post and Mail building on the right, noting the large digital clock atop the tower which would read 04.49hrs. He continued up to Bull Street, where he would board the 05.00hrs number 14 night-service bus which went to Tile Cross and dropped him off at 05.15hrs outside Bordesley Green police station.

So, this one morning he got off the bus; walked into the station and said, "Good morning " to the night man, to be greeted by, "What you doing here so early? It's only 03.15."

He looked at the station clock. It was indeed 03.15hrs - he realised he had been tricked.

Apparently, someone crept into his room and fixed his alarm clock. All the station clocks were put forward two hours. The security men at the Post and Mail were even enlisted to temporarily fix the clock.

Another superb example of police ingenuity.'

*

'The lolly'

‘In 1972, Birmingham City Council commissioned several statues for display in the city centre. One of these was a huge fibreglass statue of King Kong, the giant gorilla.

It was to be displayed in Manzoni Gardens from March to October. Because Manzoni Gardens was inside a huge traffic island by the Bull Ring, the installation presented certain problems regarding major traffic obstruction whilst the low-loader truck being utilised was unloaded.

On the appointed date, thirty police constables and sergeants paraded in the top floor band room at Steelhouse Lane police station. The roll was called, and we were given individual traffic posts. The officer presiding was an Inspector, a big Sergeant-Major type with a Geordie heritage and an accent to match.

He had however always suffered with a speech defect in that he could not pronounce his "Rs". One story goes that when he was a PC in the Force Control Room in the late 50s, he gave a crime location over the air as "Hagley Load at Lotten Park Road" (should have been Hayley Rd at Rotten Park Rd) which caused hysterics.

Anyway, we had our postings, and now for the briefing. Danny started off......"At three o'clock, a lolly will alive with a golilla on it...."

Well, military type discipline and fear of the Inspector’s temper only just prevented us thirty souls from laughing out loud.’

*

‘Tourettes’

‘A tale that a Detective Inspector used to tell when he was posted to Kings Heath, having just come from training school, and was being shown round in the Area Car on Nights.

The conversation went around to swearing. Who did and who didn’t? The driver told the D.I. that the office PC at Kings Heath swore a lot. In fact, every second word was an oath. He said that the guy was on duty and suggested they had their break at Kings Heath canteen which was open on nights in those days.

They ended up at Kings Heath about 1am and sat in a group having their meal. The guy in question sat at the far end of the table reading the Evening Mail and didn't include himself in the general chat. The usual subjects were covered - football, holidays, kids, etc.

Someone mentioned a retired PC who had retired and gone abroad. Nobody seemed to remember where he had gone. Somebody suggested Canada; another South Africa. Suddenly, the office man threw down the paper and said, "AUSFUCKINGSTRALIA” ......’

*

‘The Streak’

‘I was the first bobby in Coventry, and as far as I know the only one to make an arrest for streaking. This was at the Wheelwright Lane pub ‘kicking out time’, late 1973. A gang of men came out of the ‘Holbrook Pub’ and did a streak - about twenty of them. A call came over the radio and I was on patrol in ‘Bravo 4’ mini panda on my own.

I was at the bottom of the road, and as I drove up they bomb-burst and I managed to catch one - I wouldn't let him put his trousers back on as a punishment.

I took him back to M2 Stoney Stanton Road. We didn't know what to charge with and in the end, I think we settled for 'Breach of the Peace'.

He went to court next morning put his 'hands up' got a small fine and was bound over. This was when streaking was all the rage about the time of Erica Rowe at Twickenham era.'

*

'Making a clean breast of it'

'My Detective Superintendent at the time employed me as his 'bag-man' on Police Complaints.

One of the complaints was about officers 'moonlighting', i.e. earning money in their own time. If they had got on and finished the job, this probably wouldn't have come to light.

The two officers involved had been in the building trade before joining the 'Job'. They were 'employed' to alter the two downstairs rooms in a semi-detached house into one through room. They also removed the two chimney breasts in the rooms. However, they were tardy in finishing the alterations to the wiring, and the householder complained.

I was sent to get statements from the householder and neighbours. On speaking to the neighbours, I learned that they had found plaster with wallpaper attached in their fireplace. This was the day after the chimneybreasts had been removed from ground floor to bedroom ceilings!

Apparently, in this type of house, chimney breasts from both houses merge at bedroom level to reduce the thickness. Remembering that my neighbour had undertaken similar work and informed me that the remains of the chimney in the loft had to be corbelled to throw the weight back onto the dividing wall, I enquired of the householder if this had been done. They were not sure.

When I told the Superintendent of this, he got the Police Surveyors Department to visit. They in turn called in the City Council Surveyors, who immediately slapped a Dangerous Condition Order on the property!

Surprisingly, Philip Knights, Chief Constable, didn't sack them. He probably thought they would be better earning salary to pay off the damages awarded against them!'

*

'Performance appraisal'

'As a newly promoted inspector at Thornhill Road, I was called up to the Chief Superintendent's office, who began by saying, "I have a delicate enquiry for you that will test your lateral thinking skills."

Being very keen to impress, I replied, "Well I'm always up for a challenge, Sir."

The Chief Superintendent went on to explain that he had received a number of complaints from residents in a certain road that an officer was regularly parking his police car outside an address occupied by a single young lady. He would later be observed leaving in a more dishevelled state than he had arrived in.

“I need to know who it is and why he is going there”, was the task given to me.

Needing an excuse to visit the young lady, I discovered that she had been the victim of a street robbery a few months previously. I then hatched what at the time I thought was a cunning plan. The plan in place, I needed an accomplice to go with me on my visit, so I called a trusted ‘character’ PC to my office.

Having explained the background to him, I then outlined the plan, “We will be going there to conduct a customer satisfaction survey in relation to her being the victim of robbery. I have prepared a ‘spoof’ form for us to fill in. Hopefully if we are friendly with her, we might get to the bottom of who her ‘gentleman caller’ is.”

In the car on the way I waxed lyrical about how this was sensitive, and we would have to be very careful how we spoke and tried to get our answers. I said I would take the lead and all my colleague really had to do was be a witness to events.

On arrival we approached the front door, which had a frosted glass panel in the top half. I rang the bell and the door was answered promptly by an attractive young lady.

Before I could speak, she said, “Oh, I saw your silhouettes through the glass and thought you were my boyfriend”

Acting friendly I said, “Oh, who’s he then?”

She immediately told me his name (for the purpose of this story I will call him PC John Doe) and went on, “I met him when I was robbed, and I fancied him and asked him out.”

Mission accomplished thinks I!

She then said, “What are you doing here?”

Unable to think up another excuse 'on the hoof', I explained about the 'customer survey' for the robbery. We were invited in, made lovely cups of tea and she sat very politely whilst I went through the charade of filling in the 'spoof' customer survey. Having filled out the form, keeping up the story, I turned to my PC colleague who had, (as instructed), remained silent throughout and said to him, "Any last questions?"

This was a big mistake. He could not resist the temptation. With a deadpan face he asked, "On a scale of one to ten, how would you rate the performance of PC Doe?"

I nearly choked on my tea, but the response was even better: "Oh, about a six".

We managed to leave without cracking up and I reported back to the Chief Superintendent.

PC Doe was suitably dealt with but perhaps his biggest punishment was being known as '6' thereafter. Like I said, the PC I took with me was a 'character'!'

*

'The wrong trousers'

'Many moons ago a Detective Chief Inspector had to go down to London for an important meeting with the Metropolitan Police. He travelled by train as he expected to have a few beers with some old pals after the meeting.

The meeting over, the second part of his day went as planned. As it started getting dark and he was suitably refreshed he made his excuses and left in a state of merriment to catch the Tube, then the train.

All was going well until he stepped off a high kerb. There is no polite way of describing this, but as he stepped down there was a breaking of wind, accompanied by a sizeable 'follow through'.

He was now in Central London, with severely messed underwear and in a state of funk, with seconds before it might be noticeable through his trousers.

Walking with his briefcase behind him, covering his nether regions, he had almost got to the Tube when he passed a market stall selling clothes. He forced his way through the rugby scrum at the front of the stall and examined the wares. "Bingo!" he thought, and pointed to the cheapest jogging bottoms hanging up at the back of the stall and said, "Those please!"

Fumbling for his cash, he finally managed to pay and got hold of a plastic bag containing his purchase.

The next fifteen minutes were purgatory as he travelled by Tube then walked to his platform, feeling desperately uncomfortable, fearing being smelly and visibly noxious.

As luck would have it, his train was on the platform and he climbed aboard and locked himself in the first toilet he came to. Breathing a huge sigh of relief, he started to clean himself up as the train pulled out of the station.

Not wanting to leave any evidence in the toilet, he managed to shove his soiled clothes out of the toilet window, finished swabbing himself down and turned to the plastic bag containing his purchase. He reached in and pulled out….. a T-shirt!

He was now in his suit jacket, shirt and tie, but naked from the waist down, with only a T-shirt for modesty. His head now pulsating with panic, and sobering up very rapidly, he decided to spend the journey in the toilet. He had several people knocking the door and he resorted to shouting, “I’m not very well”, to send them away.

Luckily, he did have his mobile phone and contacted his wife to pick him up from his station.

He waited for his station to be announced and then waited as long as he dare before making the dash to get off the train.

His wife had almost given up on him; the rest of the passengers at their stop having long since cleared the platform. Then she spied the form of her husband running towards her car, briefcase in hand, with his bare legs through the armholes of an upside-down T-shirt!!

Needless to say, he had some explaining to do. Who says the life of a DCI isn’t stressful ?’

*

‘A horse with no shame’

‘I remember the mounted section on match days at the Wolves matches, I was standing having a break eating a burger by one of the horses at one match, when I felt something grab the burger. I turned around to see the burger disappearing down the horse’s mouth. The mounted officer looked at me and said, “don't feed him that he's a vegetarian” - good times!

*

'Turning the tables'

I had a habit of getting to the pre-match briefings at the last moment. In the old briefing room at the Molineux there was a table at the back of the room with one of its legs missing. I got used to the missing leg being at the back, so I used to rush in at the last moment, throw my equipment on to the table, and sit myself down balancing on the front of the table.

Anyway, the one day I did my usual trick, arrived late, jumped on the front of the table to find some wit from 'G2' had turned the table around.

The Chief Superintendent was just about to start the briefing when the table collapsed depositing me and my equipment on the floor. The briefing room erupted in laughter and the Chief Superintendent looked at me said "Are you hurt?"

I said, "No sir." and he replied, "You will be if I come over there, get on your feet and see me after the briefing!"

I was never late again.'

*

'The getaway driver'

'A senior officer was escorting Douglas Hurd and they got too close to the Handsworth rioters. He hustled Mr Hurd into the nearest police carrier with only one PC in it - 'Drive', the senior officer ordered, and the 'Bobby' drove off like a freaking lunatic. At a safe distance Mr Hurd thanked the 'Bobby' and the senior officer said he would notify his Divisional Commander of the good work.

The 'Bobby' asked him not to because he wasn't an authorised driver! - good man.'

*

'Cut the red wire'

'In 1981, during the dying days of the IRA 'hunger strike' in the Maze Prison, public hysteria had led to a sharp increase in reported possible 'bombs' being found. Most of these involved thoughtlessly abandoned bags and boxes.

Eventually, after many wasted hours spent waiting around for the 'bomb squad' to arrive, some officers developed a rather jaded view of the likelihood of any reported bomb being genuine.

On patrol one day with an officer I attended a suspicious briefcase which had been left on the pavement in Harborne. Despite having reported it as a bomb, the person reporting, and half a dozen or so interested parties, were still standing around it when we arrived. My colleague was particularly jaded this day - think we'd already been to one earlier in the tour of duty.

However, he didn't let on; instead he spent five minutes closely examining the briefcase, even lying down on the pavement to 'check it out thoroughly'. He then concluded, out loud to all assembled, that it bore all the hallmarks of an IRA device. The onlookers hushed and looked aghast, but still didn't think it was time to leave.

My colleague then announced that he knew how to deal with the briefcase and promptly threw it up in the air, launching it up and out into the road. People screamed. Some ran. The briefcase burst open spilling its contents to the wind and traffic.

At this point a flustered guy came out of a nearby building to retrieve his thoughtlessly abandoned briefcase, which he had lifted from his car boot onto the pavement, and then forgotten to pick up after locking his car.

At this very point a bus, a number 24 I think, gave the already dented briefcase the 'coup de gras', crushing it beneath its wheels.

After a brief lecture the briefcase owner was most grateful that he wasn't going to be arrested for the 'hoax bomb' and there were no complaints all round!'

*

'Elemental'

'We were on a set of nights at Stechford during a really cold snap. One of those that really should have known better went on and on, and bloody on, about the marvellous new heated windscreens that Ford had brought out and how, in his new Ford Orion, he was well away in the morning whilst the rest of the Unit were scraping and de-icing.

This lasted a few nights until the 'office man' went out every twenty minutes or so with a bowl of cold water and poured it down the windscreen and door locks of this car. The ice must have been about 2" thick come 7am. It took said officer an hour to get away. Bizarrely we never heard another thing about heated windscreens.'

*

'Spinning classes'

'There's a story that 'spinning' became so bad at Tally Ho Police Training Centre, that the senior officer in charge had to gather a cohort into the lecture theatre, to remind them of the virtues and ethics of being an officer, combined with professionalism.

On concluding this lecture, he was in the process of leaving the lecture theatre, when someone spoke up, saying "excuse me sir..." which caused the officer to become massively irate and re-ran the tirade at the gathered masses.'

(Spinning is the little known art, beloved of the Operational Support Unit in particular, of causing someone to turn around by any means bar using their name. Legend has it that her Majesty was once 'spun'…)

*

'Jacking off'

'One from Acocks Green from the late 80's surrounds a certain Sergeant who brought his new 'pride and joy', a Ford Sierra, to work and was showing it off in the back yard to anyone and everyone. Unbeknown to him some 'wag' got a trolley jack and lifted the back axle up about 1" off the ground.

At the end of the shift the Sergeant jumped into his car to set off home but because the Sierra was rear wheel drive no matter what gear he tried, or how hard he revved it, nothing happened. After a lot of cursing our intrepid Sergeant enlisted the help of some mechanically gifted colleagues (who were all in on the blag) for advice.

Finally, he was told by one of them, "Try putting the handbrake on fully, stick it in 1st gear, build the revs up to the red line then release the handbrake and dump the clutch".

Of course, the jack had now been lowered and after following the instructions to the letter our hero shot out of the back yard like an Exocet missile and was last seen shouting "Thanks lads!" as he careered off up the road!'

*

'Dustin'

'As a SOCO in the 80's and 90's we attended stolen vehicles that had been recovered to station yards.

I attended Ladywood Police Station one day to examine a red Morris Marina estate car. I found one in the yard and started covering it in aluminium powder. I had just done one side when an officer came up to me and stated that I was in deep trouble as the car I had turned grey was the shift sergeant's car. The real stolen vehicle was hidden from my view parked between two police carriers.

It took me more time to clean the Sergeant's car than to examine the right car.

I was never allowed to forget this incident - moral of story - look at the registration number.

Another story about aluminium powder - a colleague of mine once dropped a complete pot of powder accidentally into a toilet. His second mistake was to flush the toilet and what can only be describe as a 'Mount Vesuvius' of powder in bubble form slowly started to grow from the pan. Further flushes just caused the column of bubbles to increase. We fought the dam thing for over an hour with washing up liquid - the answer to all messes caused by the powder, but at first with little success.

The householder looked on in horror. Finally, we left the house exhausted. I bet that householder never let another SOCO into their house.'

*

'Sand gets everywhere'

There was once a very fit officer who prided himself on the speed at which he cycled to work, and was wont to talk about it. As usual this was a big mistake and soon a cunning plan was hatched. During a set of nights – seven shifts in those days, whilst the officer was out on patrol, some wags put sand in his bicycle frame, making it heavier. But they made sure that they prolonged the blag, putting a little more in each night. The bike became heavier and heavier and the officer began to struggle and sweat on his journey, puzzled that his fitness level was declining fast

*

'The boring tool'

'Here's one from Birmingham City Police days on the 'B' Division. In the summer of 1966, I was attached to the Accident Enquiry Squad at Kings Norton.

One day I was out on enquiries and driving along Bell Hill in Northfield. There I spotted the old radar car (A40 Farina) and as I'd never seen how the radar worked, I stopped to speak to the operator.

Whilst he was showing me how it functioned the speed needle shot up to well over the speed limit. The operator radioed the car details to the Police motorcyclist further down the road for the car to be stopped.

I immediately recognised that the car was that of a fellow member of the Accident Enquiry Squad. He got stopped and a warning was issued.

Back at the office I wrote out a message for the officer, allegedly from the Divisional Inspector, directing the officer to contact him to arrange for him to see the Divisional Chief Superintendent urgently regarding his speeding in Bell Hill.

When the officer arrived back and read the message, he went ballistic and told us what had happened. He said that the police motorcyclist who had warned him had said that would be an end to the matter.

Anyway, he rang the Admin Inspector to arrange an appointment with the Chief Superintendent. Of course, the Inspector knew nothing about it and only as the officer tried to explain the background, combined with me now collapsed over my desk with laughter did the officer realise it was a blag, although he didn't know how it could have happened.

I made a run for it and was almost through the office door when I heard a loud thud. The officer had picked up one of the bradawls that we used to push holes through files to enable them to be pinned together and had thrown it at me.

I looked back and there it was firmly stuck in the edge of the door - I kept running!

In 1983, seventeen years later I was the Chief Inspector at Bournville and on one of my visits to Kings Norton found myself in that same office. I looked at the door and still, all those years later, the hole that the bradawl caused was still clearly visible on the edge of the door. When I went back to the 'B' division as Deputy Divisional Commander in 1991, the hole was still there after 25 years.

The officer and I remained good friends.'

*

'A Marmite moment?'

'One story from the old 'C' Division. The 'event' was from before my time but the account of it was still in circulation when I joined. It concerns the police station at Kenyon Street in the jewellery quarter.

The station also had quarters on the upper floor in which the Sub-Divisional Superintendent lived. By all accounts he was a very 'old school gaffer' with a particularly brusque manner when addressing the lower ranks.

One thing he did, which particularly rankled, was that every morning he would descend from his quarters into the front office and utter loudly the single word "Toast".

All the regular front-office men knew this to be a specific order for them to make him some toast (and tea) and take it up to his quarters. No pleasantries were ever exchanged, just the single word "Toast" - and no thanks either when it was brought up to him.

One office PC had a growing and festering resentment towards this morning ritual, particularly towards the complete impoliteness of it all. But he had an idea for some redress.

After the "Toast" command had been issued, he would take two slices of bread out to the stray-dogs kennels at the back of the station.

Once there he would (I'm sure you can guess what's coming) 'wipe' an unmentionable area of the dog's anatomy with the bread. He would then toast it and provide it with a smile (more of a smirk really) to the Superintendent.

This apparently went on for some time, but the P.C. was well-known for being a bit of a 'rascal.'

*

'Squaring the circle'

'One incident I was involved in, with a somewhat comical ending, was a pursuit. On my way to 'Nights' at Ladywood, and driving into City along the Hagley Road, I passed a Ford Fiesta being driven furiously in the opposite direction.

Behind it was a pursuing police Austin Metro, blue light flashing.

Around half an hour later, pulling out of Ladywood yard at the start of my night shift, a Force Control Room radio broadcast came over the radio; the pursuit was now heading back into City on the Hagley Road.

Within minutes I joined the pursuit ,with the Fiesta, now on three wheels, half bouncing, heading toward Winson Green.

I was, however, somewhat distant from the Fiesta, which had picked up more pursuing vehicles; from three Birmingham Divisions, Western and Central Traffic, West Mercia, after a brief spell in the countryside, and at least two dog vans -around fifteen police vehicles in total.

Shortly, the Fiesta entered the estate on Lodge Road, beside H.M.P. Winson Green, and then drove in circles around a quadrant, if that's possible, of streets, looking for a place to bail out.

These 4 roads were not long ones, and at times the Fiesta would have been pulling out into a road in sight of, and before the tail-end police vehicle had turned off it, almost finding himself as part of the police convoy.

As a result, the driver, aged sixteen years, did bail out, but was rather easily apprehended.'

*

' One careful owner'

'Whilst on foot patrol I attended a report of an abandoned vehicle. It was a 1975 light blue 3 litre Ford Consul GT and it was a stolen vehicle. A cursory examination revealed it had been 'barrelled', with a penknife still jammed into the ignition.

It started first time, sounded great, and was otherwise undamaged. I called this information in.

It was customary back in the day to wherever possible, recover 'found' vehicles to prevent them being 'nicked' again. As I was just two streets from the police station, the controller suggested I drive it very carefully to the rear station yard for collection by the owner.

One street from the station, a pursuit came over the radio which was happening not that far away. I rather rashly got a bit involved in it. As I was driving by far the most powerful vehicle, it wasn't long before I was right up the 'chuff' of the fleeing vehicle - a two litre Ford Capri.

The Capri drove onto wasteland beside the Brookfield estate in Hockley, and I followed. The going was rough, to say the least, as there were dips and pathways all over the place.

Eventually the Capri slid into a major dip and couldn't get out. Seconds later I ploughed into the dip too and it stopped the Consul in its tracks.

After the arrested Capri driver had been carted off back to the station, I, and a few others pushed the Consul onto level ground, and I started it up.

There was quite a lot of blue smoke, and steam. The once magnificent engine roar was now more like the 'stuttering, hackneyed bark of an octogenarian in a sanatorium'. It did, however, still drive - just.

The front grille, bumper and number-plate remained in the dip.

Later that day, the owner of the Consul, who had been appraised of the condition of his vehicle prior to the pursuit, was somewhat flummoxed by its condition when he came to collect it.'

*

'One in For D & D'

'Birmingham City Centre. We were sitting in the van, waiting for the clubs to turn out, and a drunk 'bimbled' over and asked the Sergeant, "Is this where the bus goes from to such and such?"

"Yes." replied the Sergeant.

"Do you know how long it will be?" asks the drunk.

"About twenty-five feet." replies the deadpan Sergeant.

"Oh, you're a funny cunt!" responds the drunk.

"Uniform Alpha Foxtrot Control, one coming in for D&D!"....'

*

'More Spinning'

'There were important rules about 'spinning', and they were taken very seriously.

I remember a certain senior officer giving a half hour lecture on it to a bunch of 'cardboards' (Special Constables),at Tally Ho! It was hysterical.

In cases of emergency where it wasn't a spin you called 'Official' which was short for 'Official No Blag'. This prevented the problem of 'crying wolf' if it really was cracking off in some way.

It was sacrosanct that if you called 'Official' then it wasn't a 'spin'.

I never witnessed anyone breaking that rule.

The only time I got spun was after I was promoted and I was in Stephenson Street in the City when a certain Superintendent, who is credited with starting it all, got me with a very subtle spin.

Police folklore has it that he spun Brian Clough and HM The Queen, but I don't know if that's true.

I even taught my kids how to do it when they were young. It kept them quiet on long journeys looking for 'bods' for me to beep the horn at, and wave, and for them to be in hysterics when the unknown person waved back - childish I know, but good fun., and it whiled away those hours sat in the police van waiting for something to happen.'

*

'Supreme reversing'

'Another good one was if there were three or four of you in a 'firm's' vehicle and the driver was reversing, someone would shout "STOP". The brakes got slammed on and the remainder would then respond, "IN THE NAME OF LOVE" - brilliant bit of blag'

*

'Musical spin'

'I went on a crime prevention course up North. Officers from all over were there and they were not used to the West Midlands Police 'blagging', and the art of 'spinning' in particular. I explained the gist and that saying 'Er' was the easiest one to begin with. One of the group's name was IAN .... and I kept spinning him with his name with a song ... what was the song? ..... "Ian heavy - he's my brother" ....'

*

'Car fun'

'Back in the mid-sixties when working from Belgrave Road we would drive around Balsall Heath in an old A40 which had been turned into a Panda car. It had a little 'foible', you could pick up speed, turn off the ignition then after a short while turn it back on and there would be an almighty bang.

People in the street would jump, and dogs and cats would run a mile - tears of laughter.

Similarly, when on the Operational Support Unit the driver would turn the windscreen washers sideways, pointing at the pavement, and when near to the pavement and travelling slowly would press the windscreen washer at people on the pavement.

The officers would then look up to the sky and hold their hand out as if it was raining.

The Inspector should not have allowed it but what could you do when there was a 'belly full of laughter' from the guys in the back.'

*

'Clubbing together'

'One of the most notorious 'blaggers' was a CID officer I worked with - you never believed anything he said! The 'Mermaid' pub on the Stratford Road was a favourite haunt of Sparkhill CID - the licensees were very good friends.

One night the CID officer and a few others visited for a couple of pints.

Suddenly, a tear rolled down the officer's face and the licensees asked what was up.

Fearing the worst, I backed away as he came up with this story that his wife had a club foot and he didn't know how he was going to afford the operation.

Without embellishing the story further, suffice to say he was given a rather large vodka, the exact result he was after.

A week later I popped into the 'Mermaid' for a pint only to be presented with £40 that they had raised in the pub for this non-operation.

Obviously, I couldn't accept it and had to tell them it had been a 'wind up'.

Although the husband forgave him his wife never did.

*

'A blag too far'

We had organised a 5am dawn swoop in Hall Green and had finished the briefing when the same CID officer came in and told us there had been a murder in Armoury Road, Small Heath and to follow him there.

Of course, we all believed it was a 'wind up' so we just went and carried out the raid, and arrested the offender, whilst he was left standing on his own at the scene of a real murder in Armoury Road.' 'crying wolf' springs to mind.

*

'Not going cheap'

'I joined the West Midlands Police in 1987 and I am still serving nearly thirty-three years on. When I joined, I was posted to what was then the D3 subdivision working from either Erdington or Kingstanding Police stations.

I had the time of my life and still am.

In the early 90s, when we used to work the seven-night shift pattern, a colleague and I were assigned to plain clothes proactive mobile patrol due to the amount of burglaries and car thefts we had in our area.

Nine times out of ten I would be working with the same officer, we hit it off together as soon as he joined the Force, both of us former soldiers, we had a lot in common and the same sense of humour.

Every set of nights we would go to the Transport reception at Park Lane and 'blag' a plain car out of them, telling them that it was needed for an operation, but in the end they got wise to the 'blag request reports' and we were just allowed us to use the cars.

One night we were driving around the streets of Erdington when a call came in from our control room asking us to attend the canal embankment on the Kingsbury Road, Erdington near to the old Showcase Cinema. A security guard from a nearby factory had seen two well-built, skin-headed, tattooed-covered males go onto the embankment with a shovel, dig a hole, place something white into the hole and fill it in again.

These two individuals had then walked back across the Kingsbury Road where there were a group of shops with flats above them and gone into one of the flats.

We made straight to the location in the plain car whilst one of our 'Zulus' (Area Car) went and obtained details from the security guard.

It wasn't long before the fresh mound of recently dug up earth was found.

We borrowed a shovel off and set about digging up the fresh earth.

After a short time, we saw a white canvas package - was it gold, was it cash or was it drugs?

I removed the package from the hole, it was very light, I opened it very carefully and
I could not believe it. I opened my hands and revealed the contents of the package - two dead budgerigar's!

Well we all fell about laughing, something the two skins-heads were unable to do when they got up the next morning and found the two birds on their door mat after I had posted their property back to them through their letterbox.

*

'Dog days'

My late father Ron Woollaston or 'Woolly' as he was known, was a British Transport Police officer for thirty-three years. As a child he grew up in the 'war years' where money was short, and you collected anything you could as everything had a value, or could be reused.

As kids he and his mates would stand by the railway embankment in Witton, Aston and throw stones at the passing steam trains. The stoker in turn would then get his own back by throwing lumps of coal back at them.

Once the train had disappeared, they would collect all the coal up, share it out, then take it home.

He often spoke about collecting orange crates to re-use the wood to make things, he could turn his hand to anything.

If you ever checked my dad's trouser pockets, they would be full of things like nails, screws, nuts, bolts, washers and elastic bands, most of these were items he found whilst exercising his police-dog on the local streets of Kingstanding where we grew up.

My dad's theme of collecting was known to all the BTP officers at New Street Station, and other surrounding stations, but I will come back to that shortly.

In the late 60s early 70s, the wages of a police officer were very poor, in fact it was said during this period a dustman earned more than a police officer.

We never had a telephone or a car - we couldn't afford one.

As a family of seven when it came to holidays dad used to hire colleagues' caravans all over the place until the family discovered Guernsey, going on a Sealink ferry across the channel, but it was still down to the money whether we could go or not.

We would all turn up at New Street with our holiday belongings packed into our suitcases.

We would wait in the long dark walkway at New Street whilst dad went to the police office to collect his wages and to see if we had enough to go to the Channel Islands for our holidays.

Dad would then emerge for the police office stairwell shouting "yes we can go", but I knew that there were times when colleagues would club together so that their mates could sometimes go on holiday when they couldn't afford to.

Due to free travel on British Rail and the Sealink ferry it used to cost the family £4.00 to get from Birmingham to Guernsey, but in those days, it was still a lot of money.

With no telephone or transport, if the office wanted to contact Dad for an urgent job, or to work overtime, they had three methods of contact, namely by ringing Mrs Wagstaff at the top of the road when she would send one of her eight children down to pass the message on to dad, or by ringing Mrs Goody over the road to pass a message on, or sending a car out to our house from New Street.

My father would always use public transport to travel to and from work in those days. He would travel in 'half-blues' with a raincoat covering the top half of his uniform. He would take his police dog, which I think was 'Brutus' at the time, on the top deck of the bus.

One day a lady was sat in front of dad, she kept turning around and looking at him in disgust.

She finally turned around and without warning slapped my father around the face.

When my father asked the reason why she had attacked him she replied, "Keep your hands to yourself!"

It was then that my father realised on looking at 'Brutus' that his tail was wagging, and it was passing between the seat in front of him and would have been stroking the woman's backside - they then both saw the funny side of the situation!

In the early days of Dad being a dog handler, with life-time friends and fellow handlers Frank Street, Ivor Kerslake and Alan Moorcock to name just a few, they used to attend garden fetes and open-days at schools displaying their dogs to give the public re-assurance of the animal's demeanour.

I can remember as a 10 or 11 year - old, my brothers and I putting this long padded sleeve thing on our arms and having to run at high speed across an open school field in front of the crowds and then being taken down by a police 'land shark', it was great fun.

As I mentioned earlier Dad like to collect wood and things like that, New Street station and surrounding areas were undergoing massive building regeneration in the late 60's and early 70's. To my father it was like Christmas, with offcuts of timber everywhere.

The BTP used to have an old van, if I remember correctly, that they used to transport the dogs around in.

When the rear doors were opened you could hardly see the poor dog for timber.

All the timber would be off- loaded onto our front garden and then the following morning it would be taken round the back garden and stored in a massive police dog kennel.

Later dad was posted to the newly built, but not completed Birmingham International Railway Station. He said it was like 'dying and going to heaven', there was wood everywhere.

One night whilst on foot patrol he saw a skip on site, and someone had discarded a sheet of plywood into it.

When he was trying to recover the plywood, he had the shock of his life. As he lifted the sheet of timber up and looked underneath, he saw the severed head of a horse. He left hurriedly!

For some time, he was worried that he had found the remains of the world-famous champion racehorse 'Shergar' that had recently been stolen in Ireland, but later he realised that the horse was too small to be a racehorse.

He was not happy at all about leaving that sheet of plywood behind.

When my father passed away the late Frank Street did a reading at his funeral service.

Two of the things Frank mentioned and everyone laughed and clapped about, "I never knew anyone could get some much swag into a green duffel bag, Ron was the only person who, when late for work at Birmingham International, could dodge all the security cameras at New Street Station, board a train, arrive at International and go straight on patrol as if he had been there all day.

That was my dad all over, great bloke and really miss him.'

*

'St Trinians?'

'I was once blagged into dressing up in a school uniform, (I am female), and walking round Alcott Woods, every lunchtime for a week in an effort to catch a 'flasher'. The job was genuine enough but my then gaffer thought he'd liven things up! Not sure for whom!

I often wonder if he'd have progressed as far as he did if I'd let that one slip!'

*

'Is that a bankroll in your pants, or....'

‘On the day of the riot at St Andrews football ground on the 11th May 1985 I was Custody Officer at Bromford Lane doing four hours extended overtime after a 6am-2pm shift. I had a phone call telling me Stechford was full and asking me if I could I take a few more prisoners - no problem I said.

Then about thirty to forty prisoners arrived...most with head wounds, drunk and still wanting to fight!

I had a mature female Special Constable helping me list property etc.

One smiling, bleeding Leeds fan was only wearing his underpants...and something didn’t look right.

I told him to drop his pants and he had £150 in notes wrapped by a rubber band around his manly bits.

The Special screamed and ran out – I never saw her again and apparently she resigned on the spot....’

*

‘Oh Dear’

‘I found an old lady wandering round Wednesbury town in the early hours of a very cold and frosty morning. With all the care, and tenderness we could muster collectively we identified a house in Churchill which the old lady pointed out was hers.

She hadn't got a key, so I forced entry causing minimal damage and turned the lights on and settled the 'old dear' in her chair. I was rather pleased with myself and my good deed until she said with total sincerity, "I don't think I live here." …'

*

'Scuttled'

'When I was working in uniform in the 70's, the Mander Centre in Wolverhampton would sometimes provide a spot of light relief in the early hours of a night shift when it had gone quiet. Officers became adept at 'Tesco Supermarket' trolley races in the malls.

From the Centre you could always get back out onto the streets very quickly if the Duty Inspector called.

On one occasion when this happened to an officer, he gave a specific location and the Inspector said he would meet him there. Purely by chance when he got there, he found a dead body. The person had apparently fallen from the car park of the shopping centre in what was believed to be a suicide.

On another occasion I was out in the back of a panda one night, having been on foot patrol. The cars were not supposed to be doubled-up and I was spotted by an Inspector from an adjoining sub-division even though I ducked down.

There then followed the scene of one police car being chased by another police car until we eventually gave up and pulled over. I got one telling off at the scene and another from my own Inspector when I got back to the station.

In 1978 I was appointed as a Detective Constable at Dunstall Road, Wolverhampton and it was customary on a Sunday morning for my CID team to visit a food-caravan on a coach-park where they did bacon sandwiches.

As we were making our way there one Sunday, I spotted smoke coming from a National Coal Board building near to the Molineux Football Ground.

We stopped and I climbed over a gate to get access to the rear of the two-storey building which also had an apartment on the top floor.

We smashed a back door in and once inside could clearly see smoke coming from the basement area where I believe they stored bedding. I ripped a curtain from over a door to put over my head for protection and started to make my way upstairs shouting to see if anyone was inside.

I could hear a woman further up shouting but couldn't see where she was located due to the heavy smoke, so I tried to smash an old stain-glass window to get rid of some of it. I couldn't manage to start with but then I found a coal scuttle and launched it at the glass which shattered. It went straight through and disappeared below.

Eventually the Fire Brigade rescued the woman, so no harm done I thought as I made my way back outside. By this time, I noticed that a small crowd had gathered to watch the proceedings and that among them was an Asian man sat on the floor, who was bleeding profusely from a head-wound.

Apparently, he had been hit by the flying coal scuttle!

We all got commendations for our efforts.'

*

'Murphy's Law'

'If you have ever been in a situation where anything that could possibly go wrong, did go wrong, in a series of connected but arbitrary cockups, then you may well sympathise with the tale that I am about to tell you.

The names of the players in this farce have not been changed. All are now either retired or no longer with us, and some I simply can't remember, since this took place around thirty years ago.

As a police officer in Wolverhampton, working nights during the autumn was never much fun. Cold, wet, grey and miserable would sum up the prevailing conditions, and this particular night was no exception.

I was still fairly new to the subdivision in Wolverhampton but had seven years' service in by that time and was one of the more experienced officers on our unit.

On this mid-week night I was assigned as crew on the 'Zulu' fast-response area car, a Morris Marina 1.8TC four-door saloon, together with another newer member of the unit, a PC with similar experience who had come to us to learn the division prior to his pending promotion to sergeant. Gary had a terrific sense of humour, and was good company during the long, miserable nights.

Around 1am we were just cruising around when the radio crackled into life and we were given instructions to attend a silent alarm that had been activated in a local convenience store. Nine times out of ten these were false alarms but sometimes they proved entertaining, as was proved to be the case on this night.

We entered the road where the store was situated very quickly, and as it's a long, straight road Gary had the accelerator pedal buried to the floor. The Morris Marina wasn't the best handing car around, but it was impressively quick in a straight line… We ran silent, as was our practice with alarm calls - just in case.

As we were both fairly new to the area neither of us knew the exact location of the store, so when it appeared at a high rate of speed to my left, I yelled at Gary to stop the car. He did so, very efficiently. He made some noise in doing so but considering the wet road surface it was admirable indeed.

If you are a burglar, the sight of a police car screeching to a halt outside your current location is not something that you want to see, and so as I bailed out of the passenger seat I could see movement inside the store and heard the sounds of frenzied activity. Clicking the talk button on my radio I announced that there were persons on premises and requested backup, whilst running to find access to the rear of the store, but to no avail.

While Gary covered the front of the store I was forced to watch as several shadowy figures jumped down off the roof and into gardens at the rear of a row of terraced house to which I did not have access – gone!

I clambered up onto the low roof at the rear of the store from the side, finding the roofing material to be covered with sheets of some corrugated material, which I rather suspect could have been asbestos.

A hole had been made in one of them, which was obviously where the bad guys had entered the store and, sadly, exited the same way. Even so, I stood watch over it just in case one of them had not been quick enough.

Yet all was not lost, as my old mate Dennis and his police dog 'Jasper' (known affectionately as the 'Crazy Carrot') was en-route, and 'Jasper' had a good history of tracking. In the imaginative tradition of all of the uniformed services, Dennis's nickname was, surprisingly, 'Chalkie'.

So, the dog van piloted by 'Chalkie' arrives, a Marina light commercial van with two dog cages in the rear.

The dog was unloaded, and access finally gained to the back gardens of the terraced houses, 'Chalkie' began working his dog.

Words such as "goo-on", and "get-im" were being uttered in an enthusiastic manner, and the dog, a rather large and hairy example of the German Shepherd breed with a dodgy attitude and unpredictable nature, was warming to his task and becoming rather agitated.

At this time, poor 'Chalkie' stepped into an ornamental pond that had been covered by a layer of fallen leaves, and pitched forward, putting his right hand into the glass of a cold frame on the ground that was also hidden by leaves. The glass shattered, of course and sliced up his hand rather well.

Standing up on the roof I saw all of this unfolding before me, and being the only witness, (the 'troops' tended to keep a wide berth of the dog when he was working), to the proceedings, I saw him hold up his hand with blood streaming from the wounds.

He called out for someone to come and get the dog off him, as the blood was winding up an already excited animal by now. I moved forward to jump down off the roof, and in doing so I went through it! I had found a weak spot but was able to spread my arms to keep from falling into the store below. Levering myself out, I continued to the edge of the roof and jumped down into the garden below.

First things first. I grabbed 'Jasper's' lead and pulled him away until we were joined by fellow officers, including a Sergeant called Keith whose nickname was "Sooty", one of whom who took over the dog-holding duties.

I always carried a clean pocket handkerchief, and it was pressed into service in binding the wounds.

Having declared the wound to be in need of professional medical attention it was decided that one of us would drive 'Chalkie' to the Wolverhampton Royal Hospital.

As the only officer who had not driven a vehicle to the scene I volunteered for this task. We'd have to take the dog van since it was the only vehicle that would transport the dog in safety.

So, with 'Chalkie' in the passenger seat and 'Jasper' in the cage behind, we set off, blue light flashing.

Soon we were on the neighbouring sub-division, making quick progress, when 'Chalkie' called out "Stop, stop, stop!"

Without question I hauled the van to a slightly sideways halt, only for 'Chalkie' to announce that he had no cigarettes, and he was in need…

We had stopped right by a 24-hour petrol station, and so I ran across to the cashier's window, van left where it was in the road with blue light still flashing, and purchased a pack of twenty from a rather bemused attendant.

On resuming our journey, I was directed on a short cut that I wasn't aware of, and 'Chalkie' turned to me, saying "You really don't know this area, do you?" I answered in the negative just as we hit the hump-back bridge.

Have you ever seen a Morris Marina van take off? It must have been a rare sight indeed as these were not known for their speed. I am sure that all four wheels left the ground although without a witness I can't say for certain that they did.

It certainly felt like it when we landed though, and the poor dog was not in the least bit impressed. Thankfully no ill effects and no reduction in speed, despite some suspension gyrations upon landing - we were immortal back then.

Arriving at the hospital I parked the van, turned off the lights and escorted 'Chalkie' inside.

After a brief examination it was decided that stitches were the only course of action, whereupon 'Chalkie' went as white as a sheet.

I have seen this man face down belligerent yobs and always run toward danger, but he was afraid of needles! I don't like them myself, but I appreciate their value and have learned to accept them - not 'Chalkie'.

He declared that he wouldn't have needles anywhere near him, so that meant that a tetanus shot was out of the question, as well.

I tried to persuade him, but it took Keith showing up to convince him that it would be a good idea.

Apparently, Keith saying "You're going to have the jab and the stitches if I have to sit on you and hold you down" counted as valuable medical advice. At least it did if you were as big as Keith was…

'Chalkie' reluctantly agreed to the procedure, and with this promise obtained Keith left us with strict instructions to me to enforce that, and not let 'Chalkie' out of my sight until we got back to the station.

So, tetanus shot administered and stitches sewn, they bandaged his hand up well and sent us on our way.

On leaving the hospital we found that the van would not start.

The battery was completely flat, as apparently the standard alternator didn't like extended use of the blue light beacon on the roof when lights and wipers were also in use.

We decided to push-start the van.

'Chalkie' declared himself too wounded to take over the driver's seat, and despite my protests went to the back, bad hand in the air and good hand ready to push.

We were thankfully helped in this by the crew of an ambulance, but 'Jasper' the dog made his presence felt by barking at the strangers next to his van.

Engine started, we pulled off the car park and 'Chalkie' declared that he needed some general anaesthetic, directing me to take him to the M&B Brewery nearby.

Following orders that I not let him out of my sight, what else was I to do but escort him there? The night security guys at the brewery were always friendly and had the keys to the social club where they would pull a few pints for thirsty coppers on nights - those were the days!

A radio call from control seeking an update on 'Chalkie's' status soon had us on our way, though, as it was actually booking-off time.

So, a fairly short drive back to Wednesfield Police Station and a quick de-briefing later, and I had 'Chalkie' and 'Jasper' safely in my own car, driving them both home to 'Chalkie's' house. His own car stayed safely in the Police Station car park until it could be retrieved.

The following night, it was mentioned to me that they had found a second hole in the roof, and they couldn't figure out why, and did I have any insight, since I had been up there? I of course denied all knowledge, since I didn't want the additional paperwork that would have ensued.

A few nights later, we were not working nights, but the burglars came back to finish what they had started, and the crew working nights caught them!

The bad guys admitted to the earlier burglary, but nobody would own up to that second hole in the roof.'

*

'The wrong briefs'

‘During the miners’ strike in 1984 I was a member of the Operational Support Unit of West Midlands Police. The unit were highly trained public order specialists and consequently were constantly deployed to assist other Police forces in dealing with the many disorders that occurred during the prolonged industrial dispute.

We worked in units of ten constables with a Sergeant in charge; this was known as a serial. Three serials were known as a Police Support Unit (PSU) under the command of an Inspector.

Several PSUs would be deployed together and in the case of the OSU there would be our own Chief Inspector in charge.

During the strike the whole of the OSU were regularly deployed together, and on one deployment a ‘blag’ was perpetrated on our Chief Inspector and a large number of other officers.

We left the Midlands during the very early hours of the morning in our public order van and drove north arriving at a large pit along with possibly fifty other serials from across the country. We didn't know where exactly we were to be used and all the PSU commanders went into the pit offices to be briefed. Following their briefing they would return to their PSUs and brief their officers accordingly.

Our Chief Inspector went for the briefing and left his uniform cap and overcoat in our van.

These briefings could be quite lengthy and Police officers have a low boredom threshold, so the ‘blagging’ would commence.

One of my colleagues stepped out of our van and donned the Chief Inspector's cap and coat. He then walked along the serried ranks of vans, opened each door, and proceeded to brief each serial in detail about where they were going and what they were to do, and be expected to do.

This briefing was of course complete fiction, but by all accounts, was very thorough and totally realistic.

My colleague returned to our van and replaced the Chief Inspector's cap and coat exactly as they had been left.

Some minutes later the Chief Inspector returned and briefed us as per the official briefing. He kept having to ask why we were all sniggering but did not receive a coherent reply.

We then watched as our Chief Inspector had a blazing row with each serial Sergeant as he tried to brief him only to the have the Sergeant and his men argue that they'd already been briefed that they were going elsewhere.

As this scene developed our serial could not contain itself and we spilled out of our van in hysterical laughter.

When our hapless Commander returned to our van rather red-faced and flustered, he saw us rolling around laughing and the penny dropped.

He stood before us and held us in an icy stare and bellowed "You utter bastards. I know there is no point asking which of you did that, but well fucking done. I intended giving a thoroughly professional briefing, which thanks to you that has all gone to shit. A fucking good blag though!" ...'

*

'The days of the dead'

'Let me take you back to the summer of 1985 and my beat attachment to 'C' Unit at 'B1', Belgrave Road.

My first encounter with death was as a fresh-faced cadet.

I've always had an overactive imagination in that department; I suppose it didn't help much that as a kid I had to go past the local undertakers on the way to and from my local park. This journey was always taken in great haste with eyes firmly fixed to the ground. It got worse the older I got, because when I was allowed out in the dark, I'd do the same journey at 'warp factor 9' fully expecting all kinds of things to jump out at me.

So, I suppose it comes as quite a surprise to you dear reader that I made it into the police force - after all the police deal with all kinds of death from the peaceful to the horrific.

In the time-honoured tradition of British policing the older cadets took great glee in passing 'pearls of wisdom' to us younger ones, with tales methinks too tall to be true.

One such tale involved a cadet/probationer (it changed depending on who was telling the story). This brave soul was persuaded by the rest of his shift to play a 'blag' on a fellow shift member. The shift just happened to be at an alarm at a mortuary.

The young lad duly stripped to his waist and climbed into one of the chiller cabinets, housing a host of bodies, "It's alright lad." One of the old stalwarts assured him, "Here have a torch it'll make you feel a bit better."

Too late he realised when the drawer shut, there could be bodies on either side!

Not wanting to appear to be a 'wus' he braved it out. Panic started to rise a bit, he took another look around, 'It's alright' he thought, 'They are dead bodies nothing can harm me in here, but I wish the buggers would get me out, it's freezing.'

He didn't have to wait much longer; his scream of fright alerted his colleagues as the body next to him slowly turned to face him and said, 'Cold in here innit!'

This story came back to haunt me when I came to do my beat patrol at the end of my cadetship.

An alarm had gone off during the early hours at one of the local funeral homes. My partner and I were the last to arrive, and being the brave and fearless soul that I am, I volunteered to follow her in.

I have a vivid recollection of walking into a central courtyard, the rest of the shift were milling around checking doors and rooms etc.

One the lads said to me, "Just check the room over there young Flo.", in apparent innocence, pointing to a door to my left.

The door was ajar, But I felt relatively safe, after all, the rest of the shift had been there for a good few minutes before me and my mate, they surely must have already looked in that room.

I poked my head tentatively round the door, 'Oh Shit' it was full of coffins, stacked on end against all four walls.

One of the other lads pushed past me, flicked the light switch and got no response. He shone his torch all around - still nothing, "All clear in here", he shouted.

I relaxed, even managed to have a laugh and a joke with the others – big mistake. A minute or so later one of the coffin lids moved to the side and a hand appeared ……. My screams were heard far and wide as I disappeared into the night.

Despite all that I managed to join the 'regulars' and become a 'pro-con' and was duly despatched off to district training school where I did not too good a job either of dealing with the dummy in the dark room pretending to be a dead body. It might well have been because the old rumour squad had been in action again that day and I had been told 'on the QT' that the body in the room would actually be one that the instructor had borrowed for the morning from the local mortuary.

Or for that matter in the delivery in training of the obligatory death message to the widow Brown. I cringe when I think of what I said – yes, I am one of the many who used the words widow and Brown in the same sentence to the poor 'distraught' male trainer.

Training School is just the start of a police officer's long journey through probation, the next step being the ten-week attachment to a tutor constable.

I suppose I had to count myself lucky that as a cadet I had seen a couple of dead bodies , at a distance, although I never did get past the first crack of the ribs on the post-mortem video, before turning a very fetching shade of green and legging it from the classroom. However, I had never actually either touched one or filled in the relevant paperwork… so when the call 'Bravo Mike Two Zero, can you attend a report of a woman collapsed at the wheel of her car' came in, I leapt with anticipation, 'Oh goody, a breathalyser.' I hadn't had one of them either.

We rolled up to a little brown mini car, parked to the side of the road, on the brow of a hill, with the mist rolling.

I couldn't see anyone at the wheel. I approached from the passenger side and looked through the window and there she was slumped across the two seats, her eyes staring sightlessly towards the heavens.

With my vast knowledge of all things dead I rapidly formed the opinion that she was 'a gonner' and voiced this to my tutor, who whilst agreeing said "Yes indeed it does look like that, but you'd best just check. I can't find a pulse – see if you can find one."

I felt the blood drain to my feet, as my mouth went dry and I looked blankly at her, "Oh, ok" I managed through clenched teeth.

With a shaking hand I reached down to her neck, "She's still warm but no I can't find a pulse either." I declared.

My tutor said, "Ok. Let's PNC the car. Find out who she is, get the doctor out and the undertakers, it's getting cold out here."

Minutes later we had the doctor rolling and we'd found that she had collapsed on the road that she lived on. It appeared to be a straightforward sudden death with no suspicious circumstances.

A short while later the doctor attended the scene and pronounced 'life extinct'. We were told by control that the undertakers would be about an hour. My tutor suggested that she go to the woman's house to see if there were any next of kin whilst I waited with the body.

I said, "I don't have to stay outside the car, do I?" and my tutor reassured me, "No its late and dark, no-one about, jump in our car and keep warm, that fog is getting thicker."

Scene set – scared probationer – me – sat in a police car in the dark, on her own, whilst tutor wanders off for what seemed like about four hours but was probably no more than thirty minutes.

Looking at this car in front of me – not a soul in sight, still looking at this car in front, wondering what if we had got it wrong – maybe she was still alive, or worse what if she'd turned into a zombie.?

I was so fully expecting her to sit up and grin at me, the doors were all firmly locked and I was planning my escape route.

My tutor eventually arrived back just before the undertakers and said, "Weird bloke that" referring to the lady's lodger, "Mind you he's contacted her sister and she will be here in about half an hour."

Finally, with the body safely stowed the undertakers, and paperwork exchanged, we bid the undertakers goodbye. My tutor jumped into the lady's Mini car and drove it down the road to her house as I thought 'thank God' - I couldn't drive in case the car was haunted.

I stayed put for a bit, waited for my tutor to return, and we drove down to the house, we walked in with faces suitably fixed to greet the grieving sister, who had arrived seconds before us.

My jaw dropped and I developed an uncontrollable stutter as I thought 'Oh my God. She has come back to get me.'

My tutor nudged me from my shock, "It's ok - this is the lady's identical twin sister!"

*

‘A Draining Experience’

‘We had vans in the 80’s and 90’s which were white in colour with red and white stripes, as did our traffic vehicles.

I pulled up at a house in Lea Bank one day to be met at the van by a woman who said, “Thank god you have arrived,” and took me to the rear of the house and pointed to a drain.

It turned out the drain was blocked, and she thought that due to the livery of the van that I was from ‘Dyno Rod’ the drain company.

We both laughed at the situation - on seeing the Dyno van arrive it was apparent that they had a similar livery.’

*

‘Bubble Trouble’

‘I was a probationer, very keen to look ultra-smart, and one day I was at home ironing my uniform trousers getting the seams razor-sharp.

My father came wandering past and thought he would give me a useful tip to preserve the sharpness of the seam. I don't know why I entertained the idea because he had never been in the armed forces or the police service.

His wonderful idea was to use a bar of soap on the inner side of the trouser crease using the edge of the bar of soap to deposit a small sliver of soap the full length of the seam.

I followed his direction and re-ironed the trousers and to my delight it seemed a top tip idea because the seam was impressively sharp.

I wore the trousers to work very pleased with my standard of turnout.

On this particular duty I was posted to accompany a 'Right To Work' demonstration. The march was from Burnt Tree Island in Dudley to Great Bridge.

In those early days we had rubber 'gannex' macs.

So, in bright sunshine the march commenced - but dark clouds appeared and then the 'heavens opened' and we were all marching in torrential rain.

The rain water ran straight off my mac and onto my uniform trousers and to my total horror I noticed that as a result of the combination of a walking motion, and the high volume of rain water, my trousers had started foaming and producing soap suds and not in a small way!

After a mile I looked like a walking advert for soap powder - the militant workers who had been chanting their cause fell silent in disbelief at the sight of my uniform trousers manufacturing foam on an industrial scale.'

*

'Listening In'

'When at Vyse Street police station, in the Jewellery Quarter, only 15/16 years ago, a 'new boy' was typing a transcript of interview. We slightly unplugged his headphones so we could hear the interview and every now and again we would say to the officer, "I can't believe he said that." disturbing him so many times he struggled to finish, and to this day I don't think he twigged it was a blag.'

*

‘Don’t irritate the old lag’

‘I was sitting in the Prisoner Handling Team office at Brierley Hill trying to do a committal (to Crown Court) file. It was about 7pm.

In the office with me were two young bobbies in their early twenties. Also in the office was a guy I was in the cadets with by the name of Bob. He lived locally and had popped into Brierley Hill to use a job computer. He was in casual ‘civvies’.

The two young bobbies were ‘pratting about’, acting childishly, making whooping noises. I wrote out a note and slipped it to Bob. I explained that they were getting on my nerves and hatched the idea of a blag. Bob gave me the nod.

I stood up and said, "Are you still a Superintendent Bob?" "No Paul, I got promoted Chief Superintendent last year, I'm working on a project team at Lloyd House."

The idiot bobbies now fell silent. The one with the brains did a sharp exit from the office and lay low somewhere, leaving his mate sitting there.

Bob stood up. "What's your name young man?" he asked.

"PC ……. Sir" he replied. I have left the name out to save his blushes.

"How long have you been in the job?" Bob asked.

"Almost two years Sir" he replied.

"Are you enjoying it? Working hard?"

"Yes Sir.” He responded.

Bob turned to me. "Is he a good officer Paul?" he asked.

“He is Sir" I said, "However he's going to drop himself in the shit with his ‘shagging’. He keeps boasting about all the women he's been bedding, waking up here, waking up there. That could be his downfall."

Bob looked at him. "Is this right officer?" he asked.

"Y-y- yes Sir", he replied.

“Let me tell you" said Bob. "Many a promising young officer has dropped himself in the shit because he can't keep it in his pants. Are you going to continue doing it?"

"No Sir" he replied.

"Good" said Bob "Carry on."

Bob bade me farewell and left.

I glanced across at my colleague.

"Alright?" I said.

"No, I'm not f...ing alright" he said.

"What's up?" I asked. "Why did you tell that Chief Supt about my shagging?" he asked.

"He's not a Chief Supt", I said, "he's a DC. Next time I'm doing a file don't make stupid whooping noises."

"Oh okay". Oh, how we laughed.’

*

‘The ‘not so great’ British institution’

‘A DC I worked with told me a story about a recidivist shoplifter whom he had arrested shortly before Christmas one year. Charged and bailed, he failed to appear at court, and a no bail warrant was issued.

One Christmas night he was on patrol around Walsall and saw a small queue outside a large department store. Their January sale started at 9am on 27th December and they had half a dozen incredible bargains.

There in the queue was the officer's man, who was clearly intending to camp out for two nights to bag a bargain.

The man dropped his head and looked away as the police vehicle passed. Steve spoke to his mate who was on earlies.

At 8.45am on 27th December the officer stopped outside the department store, walked up to the queue and arrested the man on warrant, extracting him at the last moment from his prime place in the queue - oh dear, what a shame!'

*

'A Pregnant Pause'

'One Saturday afternoon in the winter of 1983, a male officer was in uniform foot patrol in Union Street, Birmingham City Centre, accompanied by a female officer.

The male officer noticed a 'hot chick' emerging from WH Smiths wearing a blue dress and a brown sheepskin coat that would not close where a bump appeared to be stopping the said coat from closing.

As thefts from shops and stores was rampant, he applied his sadly lacking detective skills, and as bold as brass, accompanied by the younger female officer, approached said potential offender.

Ignoring all protocol, he said to aforementioned 'hot chick', "hello, hello, hello, what have we here?" whereupon he pulled open the sheepskin coat and patted the said bump!

The 'hot chic' was in fact five months pregnant and the bump was not associated with stolen goods.

The female officer, upon seeing such an abuse of police powers was about to faint as her career flashed before her eyes.

The lady in question appeared equally in shock as this brazen officer had suddenly emerged from nowhere.

The male officer, upon considering his options and thinking it would be a good time to explain his actions, introduced the officer formally to the 'hot chick', "This is my wife, I don't think you have met!"…..'

*

'Double Bubble trouble'

'The Birmingham Super Prix was on a Bank Holiday and it was 'double bubble' overtime. I was working on a team of six officers and we had a draw to see who'd be working it. I was one of the lucky three.

About a week before the event I came down with a bug so I decided to take two days off sick plus my two rest days, that would see me right.

I returned to work to discover that my Sergeant had reallocated my PH to a colleague.

I was furious and I moaned at everyone but him, but word clearly got back to him.

This was in the days of telex messages and after the event took place my Sergeant walked in the office one day and put a telex message on my desk.

It read, 'The following officers failed to parade for the Birmingham Super Prix event as posted. They should submit a duty report forthwith to Chief Supt 'F' Division explaining their reasons for the failure.'

There were four officers' names and collar numbers including myself.

To say that I was incandescent with rage is an understatement. I placed a white report in my Olympia typewriter and bashed away at the keys explaining that I had been told that only three officers were required and that my place had gone to another officer. I concluded "I very much wanted to work the event and believe me if I had known that I was posted to it I would have been there."

I then placed it in my Sergeant's in-tray. He picked it up and read it out loud to the office. With each point I made they laughed raucously. I sat there fuming.

When he'd finished reading it, he said, "Good report, it's a blag."....'

*

'Party poppers'

'There was a story about a well-known very senior uniform female officer. One day she was 'entertaining' some VIP's in the bar at Bournville. I was on the No 4 Regional Crime Squad and we were always down there 'bang on 5pm' when they opened.

She had a habit of always dabbing her nose with her hankie, and at one stage she went to the toilets leaving her bag unattended with her handkerchief sticking out.

One individual went up to the bar to order a drink and placed a condom in the folds of the handkerchief.

When she returned, she continued her conversation and, a short time later, went for the 'Prop' - as she pulled the handkerchief from her bag, the condom fell to the floor.

Without batting an eyelid she coyly removed it and slipped it back into her bag. Class….'

*

'The sociable dog'

'A former Sergeant of mine had a brother who was a social worker. He received a referral that an elderly couple weren't coping very well on their own.

He sent them a letter stating that he would visit at a certain time/date to assess their needs.

He arrived and knocked on the door. He was invited in along with the family dog. Whilst Vince's brother completed his assessment the bloody dog wouldn't settle down, it was into everything.

At one point the dog cocked its leg up a large potted plant in the corner and had a piss. The couple didn't react. 'Problems with dog' he wrote.

When he had completed his assessment, he bade the couple farewell and told them that he'd be in touch.

As he walked off down the path the elderly lady shouted, "Excuse me love, aren't you going to take your dog?"

The stray had run amok in their house for an hour whilst both parties assumed that it belonged to the other.'

*

'Hoist with their own petard'

'It was circa 1990 and myself and a WPC. We were both Probationers. There had been a spate of burglaries at a local industrial estate in the early mornings, so when our shift was on nights the 'gaffer' assigned the two of us the job of sitting on the top of a flat roof of one of the units in the estate, to watch over it.

Anyone who's done this kind of covert observation will know how mind-numbingly boring and challenging it can be just sitting in the open air for nearly eight hours, while absolutely nothing happens. At least it was a dry week, even if it was somewhat cold.

By the fourth evening, there had been absolutely no activity and we were really bored out of our skulls. In the middle of the night, as we were fighting back the urge to sleep, My partner suggested we go for a quick drive around the nearby housing estate, to wake ourselves up and just change the scenery. I talked her out of it - to leave our post without permission would have looked really bad on us, so I convinced her to stick it out. I felt we had to "prove" to the 'gaffer' that we could be trusted and relied on if necessary.

However, by the 5th evening, and after persistently begging me to go for a drive, I relented and at about 3am we took a drive around the Brookvale Estate in Aston. We were in the unmarked police vehicle and I spotted a marked panda car approaching from a distance. I suggested to her that as we were in an unmarked car we should attempt to ‘spin’ the panda crew by pretending to be a stolen car and see if we could invoke a 'chase'.

I started to drive erratically, and lo and behold the panda car took the bait. A high-speed chase ensued around the estate and as I started to pull out of sight of the panda car, I went down a dead-end. We opened the doors of our car and ducked down behind the seats to make it look like the car had been abandoned once the panda car had caught up with us.

We giggled to ourselves as the headlights of the pursuing car reflected on our dashboard - a sign that the panda car had found us and was pulling up behind us – and then heard the footsteps of the approaching officers that we had successfully ‘blagged’.

Imagine our shock when we heard the voice of our Unit Inspector as he said, "Shouldn't you both be in that industrial estate catching burglars?”

Both the Inspector and the Sergeant had gone out on patrol and it was just my luck we came across them!

As you can imagine, severely ‘slapped wrists’ and it took a while to live that one down!

There was another one involving the same WPC. I used to go out on patrol with the Inspector quite regularly and we accidentally took the wrong key set for the panda car we were using but noticed that this 'wrong' key still opened and started the car we were using.

This prompted us to think of a possible 'blag': what if another officer had this panda car - perhaps we could use this other key set to 'steal' the car away from them?

So, we hatched a plan that at the next shift, My erstwhile partner on the observations would be allocated this Panda car. We would get the Control Room to send her on a false job which required her to park the panda car at the base of some flats and go up to the 14th floor. Meanwhile, I could then use these other keys to appropriate her panda car and we could enjoy the laughs as she returned to the car to find it gone - perfect!

It all went to plan, except the Inspector and I forgot to share with the rest of the Unit what we were doing - after all, blags are most fun when lots of people can get a laugh out of them. But this time, the only ones 'in on it' were me, the Inspector and one officer in the Control Room - who sent the 'victim' to the job on the top floor of the flats).

So, according to plan, I nick the car. I was in plain clothes at the time and sped away, feeling rather cool as the youth of Nechells thought I was the heroic thief of a marked panda car - I'm pretty sure I could hear some cheering.

The WPC could then shortly be heard on the radio professing that nothing was happening on the 14th floor. The Controller suggested it was a bogus call and that she should return to mobile patrol.

Then, a distressed voice could be heard transmitting on the radio that her car had gone. This is where the 'blag' went wrong. Our 'Zulu' team got straight on to force radio to report to Central Control that a police car had been stolen. Unbeknown to me, I'm now driving around Aston with all West Midlands units searching for this 'stolen' panda car I was driving.

The Inspector called me in to the station "asap" and it was then revealed that all hell has broken loose at the Force Control Room.

Fortunately, I think the Inspector was close friends someone senior there and managed to smooth it over - but the 'Zulu' teams were not impressed.

What should have been an entertaining gag, turned into another embarrassment for me - thank goodness this time the Inspector was party to it!'

*

'A VIP Lady of The Night'

'In the early 60's, there was an increase in soliciting in the Moseley area. Because the Plain Clothes Department was a bit stretched with Balsall Heath, the Chief Inspector at Kings Heath asked the uniform lads to do their bit.

I and my partner decided that being in uniform was too conspicuous, so we hid behind bushes in people's front gardens.

A 'lady of the night' suddenly walked by and we heard her ask a parked motorist if he was looking for business. At that moment we leapt out and said we were!

Having arrested her, imagine our faces when we got back to Woodbridge Road and the Station Officer asked her name, 'Christine Keeler' she replied.
No, it wasn't the real one, but it was not too long after the 'Profumo affair'. She thought it a good idea to use the name of course, but she had us fooled for a short while.'

*

'Life on the 'E'...'

'A certain officer was a practical joker and responsible for a 'blag' at Bromford Lane, when he was a Sergeant on 'B' Unit and on a 2x10pm shift.

The Chief Constable at the time came into the Enquiry Office via the public door. He asked a 'dull request' and the joker got on the desk, folded his arms across his chest, closed his eyes and said he was dead!

Alas the Chief Constable's response was not recorded.

Many years later I was posted to the Community Safety Bureau at Stechford (now D3), so this was pre-2005. Each fortnight there was an OCU Tasking Meeting, for which the Analysts prepared a bulky document. I was convinced no-one read it and so I added a new frontispiece to the previous fortnight's document - which was duly handed out pre-meeting. No-one noticed in the meeting except the Detective Inspector - he warned me never to do that again!

One day when at Stechford (D3) I was in the Public Enquiry Office and a community meeting was held upstairs. Some of the senior citizen ladies I knew by sight and I asked two of them if they wouldn't mind playing a joke on those waiting in the public area as they left. They readily agreed. So, I open the door for them and commented, "Now remember this is the last time you can get a caution for prostitution".

The looks on those in the public area was enough to know it worked.

A Cadet arrived at Bromford Lane (E2) in the 1980's on 'D' Unit. One Sunday morning he was enticed to sit in the Controller's Chair by a Sergeant, with some basic instructions on what to do - as the Sergeant went to the WC - at the other end of the building on the 2nd floor.

Someone had worked out it was possible to mimic YM, (Force Control Room), calling E2, so they called up with words akin to: "E2 are you aware of a lorry that has lost a load of chickens on Alum Rock Road?". At the time there were many backstreet slaughterhouses in the area.

The Cadet rightly answered back, "YM Standby". Then another Sergeant called up to ask what YM wanted.

By this time the poor kid was overheating and desperate for help. All the shift knew what was happening. When the Controller returned the Cadet was very happy, though not when he was told it was a blag!'

*

'Rapid response'

'I served from 1980-87, mostly at Bromford. Whilst on a CID attachment with a seasoned 'old sweat', I was parked in an unmarked car on Alum Rock Rd. A radio alert to a personal attack alarm at Lloyds on Alum Rock Rd came in. We were parked opposite, and as I leapt from the car, I heard my partner saying, 'Slow down Trixie' - my nickname for some weird reason.

I ran into the Bank, and grabbed a man by the counter, pinning him against the wall. Arm around his neck and feeling very smug, of course until my older more experienced partner strolled in..... still smoking his pipe!

'I told you to slow down Trix, it was Lloyds the chemist'.

Thankfully the Bank Manager was grateful.'

*

'Extracts from British Transport Police Journals & 'Bluelines' (Internal Police Magazines)

'Red faces and red flannel bloomers were much in evidence in a recent incident at Ipswich Station, when an old lady was locked in the lavatory on a train.

One of a party of pensioners, travelling from Scotland to Great Yarmouth, the old lady had taken copious drafts of orange squash and tea during the journey, with the inevitable result. She went to the toilet on the train, but due to the swaying of the train, her bulk and the increasing urgency of her business, she was unable to remove the necessary clothing. After she had been away for some time, her friends fearing that all was not well called the Guard. He found the old lady on her knees in the toilet.

Failing to recognize the true causes of her distress, he took her from the train at Ipswich and called one of our officers.

In the best traditions of the Force, the officer quickly assessed the situation and saw that all the old lady was suffering from was the need to 'go' – but where?

The Ladies was on the opposite side of the station and the situation was now desperate. Undaunted, he took her to the nearby male staff toilet. Here the story might have ended had it not been that the old lady was now almost helpless.

But with great calm, and a promise not to look, the officer seated her comfortably, with the many layers of clothing out of harm's way. I have since been unable to convince him that the relief of Ladysmith had anything to do with the Boer War.

Relief for the officer however was short lived – how to get them up again?

After several abortive attempts, the assistance of the female station announcer was sought, and the old lady's clothing and dignity were restored. Why the officer could only work in a downward direction is open to conjecture.

According to members of the station staff, who inadvertently burst in on the incident, the officer dealing with it retained his dignity, and his helmet throughout.' (1972)

*

'It was 0215hrs when it all began to happen whilst I was at one of the smaller ports serving Southern Ireland.

I was in the Police Office, about to take a meal break, when the door burst open and there stood the Station Master, panting and puffing, just able to tell me that someone had jumped over the stern of a Steamer into the water.

With not a moment to lose I ran like the devil to the quayside where I saw, silhouetted in the Steamer's searchlight, the person responsible for interfering with my meal break. He was bobbing up and down in the ship's wake shouting at the top of his voice, "Let me drown."

The surge of the water from the ship's propellers, as luck would have it, was pushing him away from the ship instead of drawing him down and under.

Close by was the Royal National Lifeboat Station, and on the slipway, I could see a small rowing dinghy which, with the able assistance of one of the berthing men we were able to launch. The latter being more adept at rowing took the oars and I sat in the stern. My weight at the time was somewhere around the fourteen stone mark which resulted in the craft's stern being very low in the water.

Due to the urgency of the situation neither of us had checked our craft before putting to sea with the result that we had not gone very far before I began to feel very cold and wet about my feet. On looking down I saw to my horror a small fountain of water spouting up from the bottom of the boat. Yes, readers you have guessed it – we had put to sea with the 'bung' left out.

What to bail out the water with, that was the question, and this was where my helmet came into its own. My crew member was quick to realize the situation and I am sure that he had never rowed so fast in all of his life.

We quickly arrived alongside our desperate friend in the water but due to our position all I could do was grasp his clothing and for us to return to the safety of the lifeboat slipway as quickly as possible. It was touch and go all the way back, but we made it with the craft finally sinking leaving the three of us standing in about two feet of water.

After being dried out and getting something warm inside us, (needless to say not tea), I escorted my little 'water baby' to the local police station where I formally charged him with attempted suicide. The charge accepted I returned to the Police Office feeling quite pleased with myself but dreading the paperwork to follow.

Relieved at six o'clock in the morning, off to bed, but not the end of the story because at eleven the same morning my wife woke me up to tell me I was wanted urgently at the local Police Station.

On my arrival I was informed by the Inspector that what had been a crime yesterday was no longer a crime. Section One of the Suicide Act 1961 had abolished the crime of attempted suicide as from midnight of the previous day…….'

*

'Whilst appearing at court in connection with a football-related drunken disturbance a Magistrate asked the defendant how many times he had been up before the courts for drunkenness. He replied, "I don't know. I thought that you were keeping the score." …..' (1983)

*

'During the afternoon of Tuesday 26th March 1985, at London's busy Victoria Station, a young lady approached three casually-dressed young men and engaged them in conversation.

The female said, "Hi, are you fellows looking for somewhere to stay?"

Response, "Where have you got in mind?"

Female, "At this really great hostel. (advertising card produced) Its really together. Good food. Bar. We have a disco with lots of girls and other things too if you want them."

Response, "What other things?"

Female, "Well all the staff smoke and I can get you some if you want it."

Response, "What – grass?"

Female, "Yeah, Anything. I haven't got it on me now but if you want, I have some 'speed' you can have – well not exactly have. It will cost you ten quid."

Response, "You've really got ten quid's worth of 'speed' to sell?"

Female, "Yeah look come over here." (the assembled company move to a nearby secluded corner where a small paper packet is produced)

Response, "This is speed?"

Female, "Yeah right"

Response, "I am a police officer and you're under arrest……"

The three officers were from the CID at Victoria.' (1985)

*

'Late one night, many years ago, a member of the Royal family arrived at one of our London mainline stations only to find that no car had been sent for him by Buckingham Palace.

The Duty Inspector, seeing a medal in the offing, immediately placed his car and a driver at HRH's disposal. This was graciously accepted.

The driver, a well-known character, with a sense of humour, was duly instructed where to go, and with due ceremony departed.

As they approached Admiralty Arch the driver asked, "What number is it Sir?"

HRH entered into the spirit of the conversation replied, "It's the big house at the end of the drive" indicating the Mall.

On entering the gates of the 'big house' the driver enquired, "Do you want the front door or the back sir?"

The response remains unknown!' (pre-1985)

*

‘One of our officers from the Glasgow Support Unit was escorting football fans on board a train from Glasgow to Edinburgh.

As the train approached Waverley Station, passing Edinburgh Castle, he casually remarked with little thought, “It’s a fine castle but it’s a pity they built it so near the railway.”

Someone responded, “I agree wholeheartedly but I didn’t know that they had railways in the Middle Ages!”

On another occasion two officers from Glasgow CID went to a house in the City. They knocked the door repeatedly but there was no answer.

One of them decided to look through the letterbox and said, “There’s someone in.”

The second officer shouted through the letterbox, “We know you’re in there, open the door. I can see you.”

It took them a while to work out that they were looking at their own reflections in a full-length mirror opposite the letterbox in the hall.’ (1987)

*

‘I am Scottish and just after the war I was serving in the West Yorkshire town of Keighley.

One Saturday night, about 11 o’clock, I was duty at the forefront of the Station when a young lad aged about fourteen years ran up to me excitedly and said, “There’s a ‘fia’ in the Chip Shop. Can you do something quick.”

Being very new to the area I thought I would have a look to weigh up the situation.

Just then a middle-aged man appeared and said, “There’s a ‘fia’ in the Fish Shop.”

Without any more ado I stepped into a telephone box, dialed 999 and asked for the Fire Brigade to attend.

Just then I felt a tug on my trousers as the man said, "Nae, Nae, it's a fiat."

Then the penny dropped and realized that it was a fight and not a fire that was being reported.

I tried to cancel the Fire Brigade, but they had arrived in minutes. Was my face red. The good news however was that the sound of the oncoming sirens had done the trick as there was no sign of the 'rowdies' when I arrived at the scene.'

*

'Who was the person proudly showing off some pregnancy scan images? Indeed, who was the Chief Inspector who almost fell over when he heard they were expecting two to eight offspring. Unaware of course that they were scans of an expectant Staffordshire Bull Terrier' (2009)

*

'One of the newly-formed Witness Care Unit roles is to keep victims and witnesses updated on the progress of cases.

One member of the Birmingham team recently telephoned a member of rail staff to give him an update on the case of a man who had been charged with travel fraud and threatening behaviour.

All was going swimmingly as she explained that the defendant had failed to attend court and that a warrant had been issued for his arrest. However, with a slight slip of the tongue, instead of saying that the warrant had been executed, she informed the member of staff that the accused had been executed.

Unfazed, the member of staff appeared suitably impressed that the courts were taking a much stiffer line with fare dodgers these days.' (2006)

*

'Going underground'

'In the early 90's we had to do station checks which included Underground stations. A probationer was taken to one and told to check all the platforms.

He set off to do all these checks but before he went, he was told that Platform 9 was haunted and to be careful.

He wandered off and someone went to the control room and got hold of the PA. As the officer walked down onto Platform 9 he broadcast a ghostly noise over the system.... well the officer turned tail and sprinted out of the station!'

*

Extracts from 'Sarbuts' section of West Midlands Police 'News Beat' magazines

'Ghosts, ghouls and things that go bump in the night have been stalking the West Midlands – going by some recent emergency calls taken in the Force Communications Centre.

One man reported a group of vampires merrily drinking away in a Kingstanding hostelry – the operator wisely advised him to go home before sunrise just in case.

In another incident, a man rang reporting a presence – possibly a ghoul hiding behind a bookcase and banging about in a Dudley pub.

The caller was particularly concerned about seeing this apparition because the pub in question has a strict policy of not serving spirits.' (1999)

*

'After many frustrating hours, a Kings Norton resident finally managed to arrange for the city council to collect her old broken lawn mower and she left it outside her house, hopeful that sometime the next day it would finally be disposed of properly.

That night police received a call reporting suspicious activity in a garden in Kings Norton and two officers ended up chasing two men across a series of gardens.

Although they failed to catch the men the officers did allow themselves a pat on the back when they found the lawnmower that the fleeing criminals seemingly had to leave behind. Surely the owner would be delighted to have it returned!

So as dedicated officers they heaved the machine back to their station where they entered it as detained property.

Waking up the following morning, the owner of the lawn mower was delighted to see that it had been taken away so promptly, and she was even happier when she learned she had six months in which to change her mind if she decided that she wanted it back.' (1999)

*

'Central Motorway Police Group officers on patrol – at a time when the emergency phones were not working because of maintenance – were concerned when they came across a stationary car on the hard shoulder.

Officers asked the driver what was wrong, and he explained that he had just dropped a friend off when the friend had rung him to say he had left his phone in the car. Still not clear exactly what the problem was, the officers asked again.

The driver replied, "Well I was speaking to my friend on my mobile when the sign came up 'No Phones – Await Police' I thought you had seen me on camera using my phone, so I stopped to wait for you."

After recovering his composure, the officer gave the paranoid driver advice and sent him on his way.' (1999)

*

'An officer from Halesowen spotted the following bail condition issued by Stourbridge Magistrates Court:

'No contact with co-accused except when attending court or Aston Villa home matches' – are they short of fans?' (1999)

*

'Recently an Inspector at Sheldon sat at his desk and decided to rattle off some of the letters he had outstanding.

Picking up what he thought was his Dictaphone he commented: "Letter to be typed to Estelle Morris MP" pausing to consider his next line.

A few moments later his 'dictaphone' burst into life, "That's very nice sir, but that's your radio, this is the Divisional Information Room and we don't do letters." …' (1999)

*

'It was a quiet afternoon in the Birmingham NATO HQ and senior West Midlands Police officers were assuring their nervous 'top brass' visitors that security was of paramount importance with nothing left to chance.

Suddenly there was a tremendous crash and first one leg then another appeared through the ceiling above their heads. It was an electrician re-wiring the premises.

Wiping bits of ceiling off their visitors and trying to keep straight faces the senior officers dealt with the situation safe in the knowledge that WMP would bear a special place in the memory of NATO.' (2000)

*

'Custody officers at Steelhouse Lane were surprised at the poor quality of images of prisoners – until they realized that they had substituted an ordinary broken bulb with an ultraviolet one. We understand that there is no truth in the rumour that the officers were trying to get a suntan whilst they worked.' (2001)

*

'An elderly lady telephoned the Help Desk at Stechford Police Station stating that she had been the subject of a distraction burglary in January. She said her friend, who lived opposite, witnessed the offender being let into her house.

The caller was upset that this friend had been asked to take part in an identification parade and she had not. She was most upset as she 'had got a good look at him.'

Staff identified the crime number and the officer who was dealing with the matter and tried to give the details to the caller whereupon she responded, "Hold on, must find a pen. I'm blind in one eye and partially sighted in the other." …' (2001)

*

'The Solihull Operational Comand Unit brought our attention to a Command and Control log where an ambulance was called to a report that a woman had apparently suffered facial injuries.

Fearing the worst, officers and ambulance staff were quickly on the scene – only to find that following a heavy drinking session, the woman had quaffed more than a little vodka and collapsed.

An examination revealed her 'facial injuries' were in fact the remnants of some spareribs she had been busy munching before she fell over.' (2001)

*

'We know that jobs in the Community Safety Bureau are tough and a lot is expected of you but a recent job advert for new staff asks for more than the average qualities.

"If you are interested in applying for the job as an offender management assistant you will need to demonstrate effectiveness, immortality, and integrity!"

We would like to interview the successful person.' (2001)

*

'A former sergeant at Crown Court Liaison has been the cause of much merriment in the department recently after an unfortunate series of events.

Each night before he goes to bed the former officer is in the habit of putting his blood pressure tablet on the bedside cabinet to be taken the next morning.

One night the battery had gone in his wife's watch and needed replacing. So that he would not forget he put the battery next to his tablets.

On waking the next morning, as per usual, he jumped out of bed and took his tablet and off he went to the bathroom for water. On his return to get dressed he went pick up the watch battery, only to find it wasn't there – but his tablet still was! He had swallowed the battery by mistake.

He was due to attend court later that day, so a colleague phoned court security and told them.

When he arrived at court, he was asked to go through security three times. It was not until they asked him to go through the x-ray machine backwards and told him it looked as if he had swallowed a battery that he realized he had been set up.

Eventually worry got the better of him so off he went to hospital. On relating his story to the nurse, she told him he was ticking along nicely, and following an examination, suggested some silicon chips as an accompaniment to the battery.

The doctor was amazed at seeing a mature ex police sergeant who had swallowed a foreign body as normally this was only done by children.' (2001)

*

'A member of Chace Avenue's Operations Centre had just completed her training for 'sign language' and was keen to put it to the test.

She raced into action when, just a few days later, one of the front office staff put her head around the door to say that there was a man in reception who wanted to 'sign'.

She dashed out and sure enough a lost-looking man stood in reception.

With her best sign-language she asked him his name.

He looked blank. Perhaps her skills were not as good as she thought so she tried again.

An even more blank look.

At this point she turned to her colleague and said, "Are you sure that he is deaf?"

Being met with a shrug she asked the man in a loud voice, "What's your name?"

At this the man immediately brightened and reeled off a long Eastern-European name, followed by, "I've been told to come and 'sign' today."

Two rather red-faced women produced the bail book which the man duly signed then left.' (2002)

*

'An officer from the Family Protection Unit at Bromford was completing the Antecedents form on the computer with details of a prisoner.

Reaching the last page, she was heard to say, "I've filled in what he was wearing but in the Appearance box it still indicates no."

After everyone around had stopped laughing it was pointed out that Appearance Details referred to court appearance – not what he happened to be wearing at the time.' (2002)

*

‘While executing a search warrant in Coventry, officers uncovered a computer scanner.

One keen officer wanted to know, “Shall we switch it on to see if it’s tuned in to the police frequency.”

Supervisors have suggested a computer awareness course for the officer concerned.’ (2002)

*

‘The Force is to be congratulated on its forward-thinking equal opportunities policies – but it may have gone too far in its latest recruiting advert for the Chief Constable’s driver. At the end of the usual blurb the ad states application forms are available in ‘braille and large print and on audio cassette.’ (1998)

*

‘A Detective Sergeant at headquarters was recently involved in a trial at the Old Bailey in London when his office needed to contact him urgently. They rang him on his mobile phone, which was in his pocket, whilst he was halfway through giving his evidence in the witness box. His colleague was last heard to say, “He’s cut me off.” (1998)

*

‘While taking an important statement from a robbery victim a young probationer asked the victim her name.

“Clarke with an ‘e’…” she replied.

“How do you spell WITHANY?” asked the officer.’ (1998)

*

'A local car dealer called Solihull Control Room and asked if they could speak to the owner of a car which had been left abandoned on their premises for about three days.

Enquiries were made and an officer contacted the registered keeper of the car after it was discovered it had not been reported stolen.

When asked if he was still the owner of the car the man said no – he had in fact sold it some three days earlier to the car dealer in part-exchange for a new car!' (1998)

*

'Transcribing staff couldn't help but giggle when they listened to the following taped statement between a detective constable from Solihull North and a suspect.

The suspect had started to describe where she hit the victim, but the officer quickly interrupted:

"You're pointing quite high up there near to her eye."

Suspect, "Somewhere round here. I don't know where."

Officer, "Obviously the tape can't see that, so I'll have to describe that for the tape – you're sort of saying past the eye towards this part of the cheekbone." …' (1998)

*

'An Inspector from Willenhall OCU stopped a suspicious vehicle and requested a PNC check. The first three letters of the plate were 'RWR' but making the check call the Inspector stated it was, 'Whisky Romeo Whisky'.

Excitement mounted when the vehicle came back as 'no trace' and the Inspector duly arrested the occupants and called for another police car for transportation. Other officers arrived but pointed out to the Inspector that he had made a mistake and transposed the letters.

Undeterred the Inspector again radioed Control saying, "I want to confirm the registration number I've just told you.... It is in fact Whisky Romeo Whisky...."

At this point the PCs at the scene were laughing so much the Inspector told them to 'Lost Get.'......' (1998)

*

'Silence is golden to many people – but not to a support staff member from South Sandwell Operational Command Unit.

The office worker was in a rush and not best pleased to be kept waiting at the checkout of the local Sainsbury's café bar. The queue didn't seem to be moving at all and finally her irritation got the better of her.

Seething at the slowness, she shouted across to the girl at the checkout, "Are you going to serve me?"

"Yes madam, I will – after the two minutes silence." came the reply.

The woman then noticed a hushed silence had descended over the café bar to mark Remembrance Day.' (1998)

*

‘Birmingham South Communications Centre received a call from a distressed man saying he had locked his keys in his car and wanted the expertise of a traffic officer to assist him.

The Controller duly spoke to the Traffic Unit at Kings Heath to pass on the details, but was lost for words when an embarrassed traffic officer replied, “I would love to attend but we have just locked our keys in the traffic vehicle and can’t get in.”

After the Controller had stopped rolling round the floor laughing, the caller was advised there might be a delay.’ (1998)

*

‘An elderly lady from Solihull suddenly became very popular one evening when her phone started to ring constantly, caller after caller. The only problem was the callers didn’t want her and instead kept asking to speak to police officers.

After taking dozens of calls the problem was finally solved when it was discovered an enquiry officer, ending his shift at Shard End, had accidently diverted calls to the station to the lady’s private phone instead of the main police station at Bromford Lane.

Officers arrived at the lady’s home to apologize – just as she was running out of message pads.’ (1998)

*

‘A probationary constable at Bartley Green used the internal phone to call the front office (ext. 6666) only to hear “Hello emergency. Which service do you require?”

Guess who dialed 9-999

The same pro con later contacted a member of the public and after a short conversation asked, "Shall I phone you back. You're ringing from a call box, aren't you?"

"No…you rang me!" ….' (1997)

*

'A probationary PC on D Unit at Bournville Lane was at Ryton doing a breathalyzer practical, equipped with his dummy radio and vast knowledge of his powers under the Road Traffic Act.

He got as far as requiring the 'stooge' to provide a screening test when he realized he hadn't got a breath kit, so asked his examining instructor for one, only to be told, "I'm not here. Do what you would do on Division if you were on foot patrol. Use your radio."

You guessed it – he asked the stooge to blow into his radio.' (1997)

*

'Detectives at Wednesfield overheard the following conversation in the CID office when a WDC asked, "Has anyone got the telephone number for Wombourne police."

DS, "It's 867333."

WDC, "Hello can I speak to your Local Intelligence Officer?"

Reply, "The managers not in at the moment."

WDC, "When's he back then?" with an aside "These forces keep changing the name of the LIOs."

Reply, "I'm not sure. Can I help?"

WDC, "I've got an enquiry about a burglar."

Reply, "Well this is the Spar Shop at Wombourne, what can we do?"

WDC, "Oh, I don't suppose you can help me then."

We understand that she eventually got through to Wombourne Police and asked for the price of a tin of peas and a pound of bananas.' (1997)

*

'Just opened up on the west side of Coventry is a new computer superstore called PC World. During a late tour of duty, a WPC was covering Western Control Room when a constable radioed in, "Can you give me the location of PC World?"

WPC, "Will do. What's his collar number?" (1997)

*

'Apparently the Training Department staff are still chuckling over a certain policewoman's application to take the promotion exam. When filling in the form, she simply put a tick in the box marked 'Sex'. (1979)

*

'On a recent school visit, a police motorcyclist showed all the children his machine. They all had a sit on it and pushed the buttons. He told them about the Green Cross Code and was very helpful to the children. At the end of the talk he said to his young audience, "Are there any questions?"

A small voice from the crowd shouted, "Why are you so fat?"

*

'A DC at Bromford Lane has proved himself committed to the Force's Quality of Service ideals.

As he was sifting through a crime report the detective saw that the only witness to the offence was an Asian gentleman who was deaf and had a speech impairment. Undeterred, the DC turned to his colleagues asking where he could find an Asian interpreter who was deaf and couldn't speak.'

*

'A steady drip of water was threatening to scramble the radios and short-circuit the fax machine at a Birmingham police station. The source was traced to the office above, that of a 'green-fingered' Superintendent.

Worried for the welfare of his favourite pot-plant he had tenderly placed it in his sink, and left the tap dripping slowly to prevent it succumbing to 'weekend wilt'.

Next time he does this he has promised to remove the sink plug!'

*

'Dudley's Road Safety Officer noted with some sadness how grown-up and 'worldly-wise' youngsters had become. At a 'survive alive' event children were asked to describe a vehicle involved in an accident scenario. One wrote down 'colour grey with four hub-caps.'

The PC asked, "Haven't all cars got four hub-caps?"

The response came, "Not down our end they haven't. They all get nicked!" ....'

*

‘The Accident Unit at Sutton Coldfield received a letter from a motorist admitting colliding with another car but claiming he could not stop to report the accident as he was suffering from ‘Terrible Bowel Syndrome’.

Subsequent enquiries revealed that the driver was in fact suffering from ‘Irritable Bowel Syndrome’.

The officer said that he decided to take no further action, adding, ‘such a condition if aggravated or neglected long enough could indeed become terrible’. ...’

*

‘When describing the name of a business on the media information line a press officer said it was ‘the AK Petrol Station’ – that’s A as in Alpha and K as in Colonel.’

*

‘A probationary constable on D sub-Division was asked by a custody officer to remove a prisoner’s clothing for forensic examination and was advised to use a white suit – obviously intended for the prisoner to wear. Ten minutes later enter the probationer wearing the white paper suit asking, “Should I have the hood up, and what does the prisoner wear?” ....’

*

‘Council workmen had a narrow escape when they called in firearms officers to defuse a World War One grenade in Birmingham City Centre. The device was a lethal Edwardian bed-knob.’

*

‘A distressed woman rang 999 to say her mother was keeping her awake by making loud and passionate love to her boyfriend. The woman’s sense of hearing was so acute she was convinced of her mother’s philandering even though her mother’s house was in the next road!’

*

‘There was confusion in the Force Communication Centre when officers at the scene of a sudden death called for a tarpaulin for the body, which was hanging from a tree 12 feet off the ground. A perplexed officer in the FCC with 27 years’ service questioned “What do you need a trampoline for?” …’

*

‘A Crime Prevention Officer at Ladywood needed somewhere to park the crime prevention caravan so coned off a spot in the car park.

On arriving, the Chief Inspector, finding nowhere else to put his vehicle, parked it in the reserved spot.

A message appealing for the ‘dipstick’ who parked in the coned off spot to remove their vehicle produced a ‘red-faced’ Chief Inspector.

“I’m the dipstick and who are you?” the officer asked an even redder-faced crime prevention officer.’

*

‘There was an Erdington constable who must have been standing at the back of the queue when the brains were allocated. On one occasion when investigating a burglary at a bungalow he asked to be shown upstairs. On another occasion he asked a member of the public making a complaint what beat he lived on.’

*

‘A newly-promoted Sergeant found himself desperate for the loo but on his own looking after the custody block. Not wanting to leave the prisoners to their own devices he nipped into a nearby cell to use the toilet. But it was only when he tried to return to his duties that he realized cell doors do not have handles on the inside and he was now a prisoner himself. His cries for help where eventually heard when another officer came to book a prisoner in.’

*

‘A Superintendent was given the job of escorting an eminent Brazilian around the Force because he spoke Spanish. Unfortunately, Brazilians speak Portuguese!’

*

‘A young visitor to the Force Museum was asked how you would get a prisoner from Birmingham City to Warwickshire in the 1830s. Without hesitation he suggested – ‘Group 4’…’

*

'Aldridge Police Station was being decorated recently and there were a lot of men around wearing 'painters' overalls. A civilian typist found herself chatting to a former Walsall 'Bobby', now a DOT (Observations) squad officer, who was also dressed in overalls.

"It's a good job you can work inside whilst the weathers bad." She said.

"It doesn't really matter" came the reply, "we can always work from inside a van."

Confused, she turned to her friend and said, "What a shame such a competent officer left to become a painter and decorator."

*

'A Constable from Digbeth Police Station took a witness statement from a man and then gave it to him to check the contents before signing. At this point the man exclaimed, "I hope not!" and burst out laughing.

The officer re-read the statement and realized his error where he had written, 'I am a married man living at the above address with your wife and children.'...'

*

'Officer attends Birmingham Magistrates Court as a witness and was directed to Court number 10. His name was called out and he went inside having been directed to the box. Instead of the oath however the clerk started reading out the charges. At this point the officer realized he was in the wrong court where a man with a similar name was due for trial.'

*

'Too much Information'

'One officer on 'B' Unit, on night duty, was locked in the Telex Room at Bromford Lane, by a Sergeant for some misdemeanour and once the two doors were shut his cries for help could not be heard.

Being resourceful he sent a telex to 'ATS', yes 'All Telex Stations', along the lines of, 'I'm trapped in the E2 Telex Room by that mad ....".

Several stations responded, but the FCR Inspector was unimpressed and directed all the telexes should be destroyed.

The snag was that there was one telex machine locked away which could not be accessed - in the Chief Constable's Office. There were repercussions!'

*

'Appearances Don't Count'

'Two officers went to Marston Green when a disturbance happened in a newsagent - they had parked up outside to relax for a moment.

Noises could be heard, then an adult male appeared - in 1970's clothing, flared trousers, floral shirt etc - with his face covered in ice cream.

The male was peacefully detained and was clearly mentally ill - having walked out of a secure unit nearby.

To pacify him whilst checks were made, he was asked was there anything he would like, whilst he sat in the rear of the car with an officer. Marshmallows were supplied, which he then filled his mouth with.

Upon arrival at the gatehouse for the secure unit, the staff member who manned it peered into the car and asked, "Which one is it then?" to the dismay of the escorting PC in the back, who was known for his smart appearance.'

*

'A crack in time'

'I screwed up a little bit on a set of nights. I was on plain clothes and saw two local known persons in a phone box in an area with drug issues. I thought from previous experience that this was a 'dial a drugs' situation as they were on their mobile phones and using the call box as well. I told my partner that we'd keep watch to see if a car turned up to deliver drugs and to give them twenty minutes.

Nothing happened so we asked for back up and approached them to do a stop/search. I opened the door of the telephone box and identified myself. The guys said that we should have spoken to them twenty minutes before, which is when they were actually smoking crack cocaine!'

*

'True Crime History'

The very first Warrant Number, (No 1), was given to PC William Atkinson on the 29th September 1829. This was the foundation day for the Metropolitan Police. PC Atkinson did not have a long police career however as he was dismissed only four hours into his first day on duty for being drunk.

The second Warrant Number 2 was given to PC William Alcock who was dismissed a couple of hours later the same day for drunkenness.

Of the first 2,800 constables, only six hundred were not dismissed, with drunkenness on duty featuring heavily. (Blue Lamp social media)

*

'Rubbing one's spectacles'

'In about 1978 I was a police motorcyclist working in the Black Country. One day I was on a 10am – 6pm and was making my way back to Darlaston when I came across a man sitting on the floor with his feet in the gutter. He was bleeding heavily from a head injury and I stopped to help him, and to arrange for an ambulance.

He refused to explain to me how he had come about his injury but directed me to a nearby ladies' hairdressing salon.

I went inside and asked the staff if they knew anything about the man and they explained that he had been hanging around the shop all day acting strangely until finally entering the shop at nearly closing time and asking for a perm.

Somewhat reluctantly they placed him in a chair and placed a gown on him before starting. Shortly afterwards one of the ladies noticed some suspicious activity by the man in the groin area. Convinced that he was 'playing with himself' one of them hit him over the head with a glass jar – thus the mystery of the injury was solved.

Unfortunately, it transpired that he was in fact just cleaning his spectacles underneath the gown.

The man went off to hospital but declined to make a complaint!

*

'A low ball'

Whilst on the CID at Brownhills, I went with a colleague at 8am to arrest a suspect who had been identified on fingerprints for a burglary.

On arrival my partner went to the front door and I tried to get to the back of the house, but found my way barred by a locked back gate. I shook it a couple of times and should have realized that things were not going to plan when the gate and the frame simply collapsed before my eyes.

I made my way back to the front door by which time a small boy aged about nine years opened the door and shouted upstairs, "the coppers are here", even though we had not actually had time to introduce ourselves.

We were standing outside with our hands in our pockets when suddenly the bedroom door opened upstairs and a Jack Russell dog ran downstairs and launched himself at my colleague latching himself onto his 'balls'. My colleague struggled to get his hands out of his pockets and was swinging himself around screaming as he tried to throw the dog off. I collapsed laughing.

Fortunately, no great damage was done, and we made our arrest.'

*

'Boom, boom'

'There's a shoplifting gang operating in town who are systematically stealing clothes in order of size.
The police believe that they are still at large!'

*

'First Day as A Cop....
Me: Suspect is dancing naked through the city centre.
Dispatch: Copy that
Me: I'll try, but I'm not much of a dancer'

*

The following is an extract from the book, *'Full Disclosure'*, which is reproduced with the consent of the author, retired officer Vince Smith

Vince Smith was a temporary detective constable circa 1995 on the 'E' Division Crime Support Unit and frequently worked with a DC who we shall call 'Alan' (not his real name), who was a regular visitor to the Biddle & Webb auction house, which is just off the Ladywood Middleway near to Birmingham city centre. Vince recalls:

'Alan and I were out and about one day in an unmarked car. At 9.15 am, we were parked outside Biddle & Webb waiting for it to open. Over the radio, details were broadcast of an armed robbery at a post office in Sparkbrook.

Being keen, I suggested that we should at least make towards the area. Alan was having none of it, and as I was in the passenger seat, he had cast the deciding vote.

I listened to the radio for updates. The description of the offender was circulated: An Afro-Caribbean male, six feet tall, with glasses, and wearing a combat jacket. The robber had jumped into his getaway car and was being chased by the police. Initially, he managed to lose them. We never moved. Alan kept checking his watch. The cops kept finding and losing the suspect. Given the sightings, with every follow and loss, he seemed to be trying to find us.

Finally, the offender's car was no more than a hundred yards away and directly in front of us! We never moved. A six-foot-tall, Afro-Caribbean male, with glasses and wearing a combat jacket ran past us. Alan sighed, and finally, we moved.

We gave chase, and as we played squash most days, we were quite fit. We followed the suspect through an alleyway and eventually the suspect turned left and ran into a National Westminster Bank.

I did not know it, but the 'Nat West' had been a hugely profitable place for him to visit on previous occasions; that was not the case on this day, though. As Alan and I chased him into the bank, I saw the suspect's heels as he ran up some stairs. Alan went to follow. I stopped him because I had actually been to the bank the week before: I knew that the upstairs area was totally secure.

We waited at the bottom of the stairs and when the thief ran back down, we tackled and arrested him. Fortunately, for us, the armed part of the robbery at the post office was two weightlifting bars that had been taped together and placed in a carrier bag, to look like a shotgun, but we had no way of knowing that.

Jubilant, we took our prisoner to Acocks Green police station and lodged him in the cell block. Alan and I went into the CID office to brag about our heroic arrest.

The local Detective Sergeant tried to not look too impressed and told me to make him a cup of tea. Alan was delighted: he had worked out that this arrest would result in our working the weekend, and that we would rake in a boatload of overtime.

I made the DS his tea and went to put his cup on his desk. In that anal way that some people try to protect their workspace from tea stains, the DS slid a recent Midlands Crime Intelligence circulation under his cup. This was an internal document that contained CCTV photographs of suspects committing offences.

There were pictures of our prisoner committing three armed robberies at the National Westminster Bank in Sheldon.

I quickly swapped the MCI for some plain paper and left. I showed it to Alan, who mentally upgraded his family's annual holiday. The offender was a well-spoken, courteous law student, who had never been in trouble with the police. He came from a decent family in Solihull. His mother was a surgeon, and his father an anaesthetist.

Alan had a different way of dealing with suspects. Instead of unpleasantness, he tried sympathy, understanding and kindness. He bought the suspect, whom I shall call Dwayne, McDonalds meals, 'The Times' newspaper and a law magazine. Alan wanted admissions, but he also wanted Dwayne to admit the offences at court so that he would not have to give evidence.

Alan's interview was genuinely kind and caring. Dwayne gave an incredibly detailed account of the four robberies that he had committed. I watched how Alan approached interviewing. There was more than one way to skin a cat, it seemed. Dwayne made one request, before his mum found them: could we please dispose of all of his copies of 'Big Jugs', which were hidden under his bed? There was no shortage of volunteers for that job.

Dwayne pleaded guilty at Crown Court and was sentenced to six years imprisonment for the robberies he had committed. Alan was delighted, not about the sentence, but the guilty plea meant that he did not have to attend court.

*

Our intelligence officer was a huge man-mountain. He must have weighed twenty stone, and could punch hard, really hard. He treated our teams' police vehicles like his own personal carpool, and once he had car keys in his hand, no one was ever going to get them from him. It pissed us all off, more than just a little.

On the Monday after our heroic arrest, Alan told me to be outside my house at precisely 4.30am on Tuesday morning. At light o'clock the next day he collected me, and we drove to Edward Road. En route, he told me that I did not have the security clearance to be briefed until we arrived at the nick. Fair enough, this must be important.

At the station, Alan led me to one of our crime cars, a silver four-door Ford Escort. As per usual, I sat in the front passenger seat. Alan handed me half of a two-pound bag of flour, a funnel, and a rag. Then he showed me how to pour the powder into the air vents on the dashboard. We filled the vents, then wiped down the car, leaving no trace of our actions. Alan pointed all the vents towards the driver's seat and set the control to maximum blow.

Alan had briefed our Detective Inspector, whose nickname was 'Bosher', who spoke to the big intelligence officer when he came on duty. Bosher told him to drop some papers off at Lloyd House. When the Intelligence man saw car keys on one of our desks, he grabbed them and said to us that he was doing a job for the boss, and added that if we wanted the car, then we could all just fuck off. We protested, he squealed with delight and plodded off to the car pound.

As he approached the car, the entire Divisional Crime Support Unit was watching through the first-floor windows: there must have been over thirty officers and staff, all waiting in anticipation.

The Intelligence officer wore spectacles and was in plain clothes. Come to think of it, I don't think police uniform has ever been made in his size, if he'd turned up at the police stores, they would have had to wallpaper him in a blue flock. We had a perfect side-on view. He gunned the engine, the flour exploded like an airbag. The entire car interior was instantly white. It looked like someone had Tippexed the windows.

He roared, then tried to escape the blizzard inside the car. He fell out of the car and looked like a pissed-up snowman. Then he blindly groped his way back to his feet using the car for leverage. He was looking for the culprits but couldn't see anything. He realised why and removed his glasses. The big man stood like Everest, white from head to toe, except for two perfectly round circles where his glasses had been.

Barely able to breathe for laughing, we ducked down at the windows. Still yelling curses at the courtyard, he stomped towards our office, leaving a thick, white smoke trail behind him. He was going to punch someone really, really, really hard.

By the time he walked into our office, we were back at our desks. Though he looked hilarious no one laughed. Alan had positioned himself next to the fire escape door.

The snowman stared at him, he was reasonably sure that Alan was responsible, but looking for some sort of confirmation before he dismantled him. Alan was fifteen feet from him. Alan made eye contact. There was a hush in the office before Alan enquired:

"Everything all right, flower?" That was enough. He roared and advanced on Alan, turning over a desk that was in his path. Alan burst through the fire escape giggling his head off and fled; he didn't come back to work for four days.'

*

John Richards. West Midlands Police 'Poet Laureate'

We conclude with special thanks to retired WMP detective officer John Richards who framed much of his humour in the form of poems which were produced at leaving functions or social events - much to the fear of the recipients!

He was also known to produce the odd 'spoof' document one of which is reproduced here. But we begin this section with some stories from John.

*

'Digbeth Days'

'Life in Single Men's Quarters at Digbeth for over six years in the early 70's was a great experience and provided so many laughs and stories, many of which will (and should) remain untold. Again 'drink' was a major factor in the day to day events.

One particular officer occupied a room at the end of the corridor and had great difficulty in navigating his way to the bathroom situated at the other end of the corridor, during the night. This was aggravated after drinking copious amounts of ale across the road in the Midland Red Club. He would on occasion manage to find the bathroom but would mistake the wash basins for the urinal.

On some occasions he would pass the bathroom completely and stand at the top of the staircase and provide a cascade down the two floors.

On other occasions he would fail to reach the bathroom and enter any available room and provide its sleeping occupant with an early morning shower!'

*

‘When I was on the Robbery Squad at Digbeth a certain officer, well-known for playing the bagpipes, had an annoying habit. He would bring food back to the office from the canteen to eat. A sandwich, toast or even a meal on ‘a plate’, which, after devouring the food, he would leave on anyone’s desk rather than his own!

Initial attempts to get him to move the offending plate fell on deaf ears. I then started to return ‘the plate’ on almost a daily basis. It would be placed on his desk, under his desk, in his desk, on his chair, in his drawers, his ‘In tray’, etc., etc.! He would of course retaliate, by leaving it in places around my desk, my briefcase, amongst clothing etc., etc. It would even arrive in an envelope in the internal dispatch.

This went on for days and weeks! He then started his stint as the ‘Night Detective’ – ahhhhh peace at last – no more troublesome plate.

I got up one morning at home, opened the curtains ready to face the day, to be confronted by ‘the plate’ strategically placed in the middle of my lawn!

Game. set and match to him!’

*

‘Another officer was also on the Robbery Squad at that time and enjoyed more than the occasional ‘schoolboy prank’ in the office. He would squirt lighter fuel across desks etc. and light it causing flames to spread rapidly and spectacularly.

He perfected this routine to reach our bagpipe player's desk as he was attempting to broaden his knowledge by reading 'The Times'. This resulted in the flames igniting the newspaper and the officer juggling the fireball around the office.

On another occasion he squirted some fuel across the floor towards another officer's desk! The fuel unfortunately reached the bottom of the trousers of the officer's new suit which I believe he was wearing to attend an interview later in the day. Our miscreant duly applied ignition to the line of fuel. Flames shot across the floor to the officer sitting at his desk. As the flames lapped around his ankles, he leapt up like a Morris Dancer on 'Speed', frantically slapping his trousers and shouting profanities!

This poor officer was the victim of another one of his colleagues' jolly japes! They put a huge pig's head in the drawer of his desk. The rest of the office waited patiently him to open the drawer and were not disappointed at his 'Shock and Awe' reaction!'

*

'I sent a well-known Detective Sergeant a report purporting to come from the Police Surveyors/Housing. It informed him that due to the forthcoming extension being carried out at Birmingham Airport, he and his family would have to vacate their Police House in Shard End and move to a maisonette in Alma Way, Chelmsley Wood, for several weeks – not the poshest of areas. He fell for it big time and had a major rant about it on the phone to the Surveyor.'

*

'There was another letter I sent to a different officer. We had arrested a prisoner on the old 'Theft from Vehicle Squad', during which the prisoner had sustained some minor injuries in a struggle. The letter purported to come from a firm of Solicitors stating that they were intending to pursue a civil action in the High Court on behalf of their client to seek substantial damages against him. He fell for it and panicked as it was just before he was getting married/buying a house.

He decided he would have to go and confess all to the Superintendent, seek his advice and beg for mercy! We had to drag him away from the gaffer's office!'

*

'I arrested a member of a well-known criminal family after two of us had found his car parked illegally on Smallbrook Queensway. We did a local removal to somewhere in Balsall Heath and on returning to Smallbrook Queensway, found the owner having a rant. I booked him for unnecessary obstruction whereupon he ripped my pocketbook in half. He obviously had to come in and with the assistance of a van, we managed to arrest him.

Obstruction, Criminal Damage and Drunk and Disorderly etc were the charges. He was represented by an elderly solicitor. He attended Digbeth and stated that his client would admit all charges against him, except he wasn't drunk and requested that he be allowed to provide a urine sample for examination.

The prisoner provided a sample and I sent it off to the Laboratory. Unfortunately, I forgot to request that it should be examined for alcohol content! The report was duly returned stating the sample contained 100mls of urine.

On the morning of court, the solicitor asked me what the Laboratory report had come back with. I told him 'Oh it came back as 100.........!' He interrupted me and said, 'Oh he's well over then. We'll plead Guilty!'

*

'On another occasion an officer was the 'office-man' and had allowed a Solicitor to consult with his client in the cell as there were no interview rooms available.

This firm of solicitors were infamous for spending ages completing their legal aid forms and 'consulting' with their clients. When they were finally ready for interview, it was always a 'No Comment' answer to everything.

Anyway, the Solicitor had been left in the cell for quite some time and started banging the cell door and shouting. This resulted in the normal Digbeth response of ignoring any such behaviour. The Solicitor remained in situ and became more and more enraged and started yelling at the top of his voice.

In due course the officer strolled down to the cell and peered in to see what the commotion was. He saw the red-faced Solicitor staring out of the trap door screaming, "I've been in here for two hours! I've been banging the door! I've been shouting! What one earth do you think you are doing, are you deaf or something?' The officer's dead-pan response was - 'Pardon!' – he actually did have a hearing problem.'

*

'A Fuss Over A Car Petrol Key'

'When I arrived the petrol key, I found to be U/S,
I'll borrow the receptionist's, he'll probably say 'yes'.
"You'll have to see the 'Super' son, for him to say OK,
I think he's in his office which is just across the way."
The 'Super' said, "There is a spare that can be used of course,
But that facility is only for a visiting police force."
That's fair enough I thought, to explain what I should do,
"You'll have to go to Lloyd House son, to get a key that's new."
I used the phone to verify that this was fine with them,
"Oh, that's alright but hurry up, we close at 5pm."
And just to make things difficult to add to that retort,
I had to get an authority on a typed and signed report.
So back I went to Digbeth on just a wing and prayer
And sought the help of typing staff who operate from there.
The report was typed and I took it in to see the DCI
But it blew out through the window, it nearly made me cry.
So back again I went to see the female typing staff,
I must admit I failed to see what made them start to laugh.
With another report firmly gripped, back I went to drive
to the Transport Office at Lloyd House, the time was just on five.
The Transport Manager was not impressed with my sorry tale of woe

And he started to tell me off, I could have told him where to go.
He checked his book and glared at me like a creature from afar,
"There's something wrong this petrol key wasn't issued to that car."
"Well don't blame me." I blurted out, "Nothing to do with me."
"Well someone must have swapped it; I know the CID."
Finally, a miracle, he granted me a key,
From a bunch of a hundred thousand he'd got hidden secretly.
You'd think that was the end of this sequence of despair,
But on Thursday morning the Transport Manager lost his hair,
For reasons that a colleague would be able to explain..........'

*

'Another retirement function'

'I'd just like to say a few words, as a mark of our respect.
I thought I'd say them now, before we all get wrecked.
No longer can you call him Detective Sergeant ....
XXXX has now become part of 'All our yesterdays'.
No, he hasn't changed his name again, no he hasn't had the sack.
He's been forced to leave the job through a problem with his back.
The doctor stated very clearly,

The injury was sustained at work and would cost the police force dearly.
But then he went and changed his mind
They reckon he changed it with something he found in his behind.
It's sad XXXX that you must go, but there's a great big world out there.
There are so many things people do – make sure you get your share….
The presentation follows now – its short – so don't get bored!
A gift from the office plus your Long Service and Good Conduct award.
In addition, quite seriously from us all at Steelhouse Lane,
We wish you all the very best – our loss is N.A.R.P.O's gain.'

*

'A colleague moving on'

'So, you're off to pastures new,
To Bradford Street, the DCSU.
Abandon ship and leave the mess,
Time to relax and adjust the stress.
Taking over from that man XXX,
And all the men that were under him,
To lead them and investigate serious crime,
And 'rip the arse' out of the overtime.
From all your colleagues and DI…………
The real detectives of the City.
We'd like to wish you all the best,
And trust you will enjoy the rest.
If we can assist you any way
Each and every day,

Pick up the phone and give us a call,
Because the DCSU lads will be doing f.... all!'
(DCSU = Divisional Crime Support Unit)

*

Detectives posted to nights were required to produce a 'night note' outlining details of serious crime and persons arrested between 10pm and 6am. This is an example of one of John Richards' lighter moments towards the end of his career:

'Steelhouse Lane CID Night Note ending 7.0am Monday 5th March 2001'
For Information

Yuree IVEGONOV B. 1/4/60. NFA (believed to be a former resident of Russian Territory of Bakusoonasican)
The above was found wrapped in a blanket packed with ice, inside a sealed container at the Birmingham Fish Market during the early hours. The container shipped from Sardinia was marked 'Not to Be Opened', however an alert member of the Security/Markets Police heard snoring coming from it.

Police were informed and managed to open the container to discover the above man in a semi-conscious state together with a small dog.

A PNC check shows there is a male with very similar details wanted for a number of matters including offences under the recent legislation relating to the movement of animals. In view of this and likelihood that this man may be the carrier of 'foot and mouth' a five-mile exclusion zone has been set around the Fish Market preventing any movement of hoofed animals.

The man, who claims to be a musician, has documentation on him which suggest that he previously claimed political asylum in similar circumstances in a number of countries, the latest being Cuba.

This man neither speaks nor understands English. He is partially sighted and deaf but is able to communicate easily in Arabic Sign Language. He is a fully paid up member of Birmingham City Football Club. He is believed to be suffering from paranoia. He has requested two solicitors (one each) and that his Embassy be notified.

Markers indicate that this man is violent in that he threw a bottle of Peroxide over his local Clergyman. (He was charged with Bleach of the Priest)

In another incident he set fire to a friend who had artificial legs and who was burnt to the ground.

Records show that he was born at a very early age. He went to a good school – it was approved by the Government. His parents were in the Iron and Steel Industry. His mother used to Iron and his father used to ….

He has a conviction for Bestiality. On the same date his brother was fined for acting a goat.

His small dog - nicknamed Carpenter (Because he's done a few jobs around the station) has been checked but is now black and tan.

Early DO can now destroy this because I don't have any more Nights to do and there is nothing of interest!'

*

John Richards' retirement speech in poetic form encapsulates - *'The Police Family'*

'I didn't get much sleep last night, because today is one, I've dreaded.
I didn't know whether to stay sober or get absolutely shedded.
As you might have guessed I've written this poem for you
It really does feel strange to say – It's my Retirement Do.
An evening touched with sadness, emotions running high,
A slight tightening of the throat – teardrops welling in the eye.
Colleagues that I've worked with, friends from far and wide
You've all turned up tonight to be here at my side.
What a load of Bobbies, it's me who'll be crying, I've just been given the bill,
It's the first time that other people's drinks are going to make me ill.
I should have guessed that it's a chance that you lot wouldn't miss,
For JR to have a function and for a night out on the Piss.

There are so many thank-you's that I would like to say,
To lots and lots of people that I've met along the way.
It's impossible to name all those people here tonight.
But if I didn't mention some, then it would not be right.
Thanks to my Mum and Dad for allowing me to come,
From the Valleys down in Wales to join the Police in Brum.
Oh yes, thanks to Anne Robinson – she does the weakest link.
She doesn't like the Welsh – well I think her programmes stink.
Thanks to Sergeant Stan – because it was his decision,
I was posted from the cadets to Digbeth – A Division,
In thirty years, I haven't moved far. I've stayed here in the City.
I've had some interesting jobs but others pretty sh...crap.
I'm sure it was Stan, as a result of what he did
That I was able to buy my cadet service for only thirty-two quid.
That was a fair bit of money back in 1971.
But what a great investment – cause my service now is done.
Thanks to Tony, my tutor, it's his fault you see,
He showed me the ropes as a young fresh-faced PC.
Thanks to Mike, who as a DS, he was the best,
For me he stood out and was far above all the rest.
Thanks to Ol' Roy for transferring me to the CID,
And to all the other bosses for looking after me.
It hasn't all been perfect, but I've really had a laugh,
Working hard and playing hard with the occasional half.

Thanks to the Complaints Department who investigated me
…………………back in 1993………………………………
Of course, it was all rubbish – they had to say they were sorry.
But as a result of the complaint, things got even more sordid.
My Long Service and Good Conduct medal could not be awarded.
Eventually it was all sorted and they gave the medal to me.
But there was no special presentation do – unfortunately.
Anyway, I'd like to thank the girl in Personnel whom I saw.
"Have you come for your medal love?" she asked, "It's in that basket by the door."
Thanks to all the criminals I've met from day to day.
Through them I've earned me some overtime which always adds to the pay.
Talking of the overtime Smudge and Dom spring to mind,
Two richer/keener Detective Sergeant's I don't think you will find.
One officer sleeps in the back office – that's strange – I'll bet you're thinking
It's because he can't remember where he lives when he's been out drinking.
He lies there with no clothes on from his head down to his toes,
At 7 our cleaner comes in and adjusts her vacuum hose.
Thank you to a couple of brain surgeons – well they only saved my life

And I couldn't have got away with it all if it wasn't for my wife.
So, a special thanks to Gail and Jenny my lovely daughter
Oh, and I mustn't forget Old Claude and Andy the Porter
Hey, its Grand National Day tomorrow Barry's on a horse,
The Liverpool get will be a good bet around the Aintree Course
I didn't realise he was a jockey, but I overheard him just outside.
He said he wouldn't be staying long tonight because he's got a ride.
To be crystal clear – after Tuesday I won't be here anymore,
At 4 o'clock, I'll be off speeding through the door.
So, to everyone in the office can I wish you all the luck.
Because after 4 o'clock I couldn't give a monkey's....
And so, I'm coming to the end of this, my final Ditty.
Thanks for all that's been said and the gifts and to Captain Pretty.
Thanks to Keith and all the Bar staff, that's everything I think
I'm going to finish now, because I'm dying for a drink.
Seriously now, I'd like to thank you all for me it's been a pleasure.
I've had some fantastic moments and have memories that I will treasure.
To everyone I've worked with and to friends and all the rest.
It's been terrific for me to have known you all and I wish you all the best!'

***

Michael Layton & Stephen Burrows (2020)

*

ACKNOWLEDGEMENTS & REFERENCES

A special thanks goes to James Myhill from the British Transport Police for the photograph he took which forms the front cover.

*

With thanks to Bill Rogerson from the British Transport Police History Group for allowing us to use extracts from some of the BTP Journals & Bluelines

*

With thanks to Jackie Harrison (Head of Digital & Engagement – Corporate Communications) West Midlands Police for allowing us to use extracts from historical 'Beacon' and 'Newsbeat' magazines.

*

The following serving and retired police officers are especially thanked for their interest, support and contributions.

*

Lindsay Adams – Retired West Midlands Police Officer
Gary Ashby – Retired West Midlands Police Officer
Jeffrey Barley – Retired West Midlands Police Officer
Kay Beal – Retired British Transport Police Officer
Graham Beard – Retired Warwickshire Police Officer
Andy Brizell – Retired West Midlands Police Officer
Michael Cresswell – Retired West Midlands Police Officer
Patrick Edwards – Retired West Midlands Police Officer
Tony Everett – Retired West Midlands Police Officer

Steve Favill – Retired West Midlands Police Officer
Iain Garrett – Retired West Midlands Police Officer
Emlyn Griffith – Retired West Midlands Police Officer
Dave Haffenden – Retired West Midlands Police Officer
Malcolm Halliday – Retired West Midlands Police Officer
Stuart Harris – Retired West Midlands Police Officer
John Hirst – Retired West Midlands Police Officer
Adrian 'Ada' Howles – Retired West Midlands Police Officer
Stuart Knight – Retired West Midlands Police Officer
Norman Langford – Retired West Midlands Police Officer
Nicholas Mathers – Former West Midlands Police Officer
Steward Mart – Retired West Midlands Police Officer
Stephen Marple – Former West Midlands Police Officer
Deb Menzel – Retired West Midlands Police Officer-member of the WMP Museum Group
Bob Moon – Retired West Midlands Police Officer
John Morgan – Retired West Midlands Police Officer
Paul McElhinney – Retired West Midlands Police Officer
David 'Percy' Page – Retired West Midlands Police Officer
Graeme Pallister – Retired Warwickshire Police Officer
Kirsty Lee Pattinson – Retired West Midlands Police Officer
Richard Pope – Former West Midlands Police Officer
John Richards – Retired West Midlands Police Officer

Dave Roberts – Retired West Midlands Police Officer
Derek Rowe – Retired West Midlands Police Officer
Janet Russell – a resident of Birmingham
Rik Scone – retired West Midlands Police Officer
Pritpal Singh Sihota – Retired West Midlands Police Officer
Vince Smith – retired West Midlands Police Officer and author of *'Full Disclosure'*
Andy Stange – Retired West Midlands Police Officer
Angie Stephenson – Retired West Midlands Police Officer
Jan Such – Retired West Midlands Police Officer
Alan Taylor – Retired West Midlands Police Officer
Michelle Taylor – Retired West Midlands Police Officer
John Thorogood – Retired West Midlands Police Officer
Ronnie Wilkie – Retired British Transport Police Officer
Andy Woollaston – West Midlands Police Officer

*

A note from the authors

If you enjoyed this book, please take a moment to leave a review on its Amazon page. It will be greatly appreciated by us. Many thanks for your support.

Printed in Great Britain
by Amazon

87348814R00079